Nobody Cares Work Harder

Terry Mills

To Dee Moon Publishing
Atlanta, Georgia
www.todeemoonpublishing.com
info@todeemoonpublishing.com

All rights reserved including the right to reproduce this book or portions thereof in any form whatsoever.

Copyright © 2020 by Terry Mills

Cover design: Kenneth Johnson
Picture This Media Group

Interior Design: To Dee Moon Publishing

No part of this book may be reproduced in any form or by any electronic or mechanical means including information storage and retrieval systems, without permission in writing from the author. The only exception is by a reviewer, who may quote short excerpts in a review.

To book Terry Mills for speaking engagements, email tmills@tmillsrealtygroup.com

Printed in the United States of America

ISBN: 978-1-7347224-2-0

This book is dedicated to my two sons,
Trace (TM3) and Tage (TM4).

Your lives have given my life new meaning and purpose. I want both of you to live a God-fearing life. My life message is for you to know life will have its peaks and valleys and no matter the circumstance you must persevere.

Pandemonium

Part of my weekly routine is to work out with my personal trainer Kevin. This Wednesday night was like most; yet, it was a night that I never will forget. "Drive! Drive! Drive!" my trainer, Kevin Brown, aka "The Trainer from Hell" yelled out as I pushed a weighted sled up and down the turf. Kevin was known for working with college and professional athletes such as Quinnen Williams, of the NY Jets and Daron Payne, of the Washington Red Skins and sometimes he would take on private clients. I've been training with him for 2 years now and every workout is hard. As I completed my last set, my legs were on fire, and I was laying on the turf, sweating profusely. I had else nothing to give, and I began asking myself, "Why am I doing this again?". Then someone yelled out from the lobby, "Are you serious!?? They just shut down the NBA season!". Startled, I wanted to jump up and watch the news announcement along with everyone else, but I was too tired from my excruciating work out. I laid on the turf until I was able to catch my breath. When I finally made it to the front of the gym, everyone was gathered around the TV. Their faces were painted in shock and disbelief. The NBA had just announced they were suspending the season after a Utah Jazz player tested positive for Coronavirus (COVID-19). Recently, Coronavirus and the severity of the virus had become a topic of conversation however, I did not think much of it until that moment. When I arrived home that evening, I asked my wife Tiquela, a nurse, if she heard the news about the NBA.

She responded, "Yes, I keep telling you this virus is serious, and things are going to get worse before they get better. People are actually dying, and the only way to stop the spread of the disease is to keep people away from each other until we find a cure."

That night the fear of the unknown kept me awake. All I could think about was my family and my livelihood, the real estate business. Everything from restaurants to barbershops were beginning to shut down. Although realtors were considered "essential", there was no guarantee that people would still buy houses. I had two choices: panic mode or stay focused and work harder. Questions such as, would the housing market crash like in 2008? If so, how would I provide for my family? I prayed and asked the Lord to cover us during these trying times. About two weeks later, the governor executed an executive order that ordered all non-essential businesses to close in an effort to prevent the spread of the disease. Things were now serious, and the country was in the middle of a pandemic. The world was terrified. Hospitals were beginning to fill with affected people. Schools and businesses were forced to close, which resulted in many employees being furloughed or left without jobs. Quarantine or "social distancing" became household terms. I had a family to take care of and a team of real estate agents depending on my leadership, therefore, I called a mandatory Zoom meeting with my team to discuss our plan and how we would adjust to the "new normal". Although I was uncertain of things I knew I had to lead by example and keep my team in good spirits.

"Now was not the time to stop! We have to work harder!" Instead of making ten calls a day to our database, we need to make twenty! The focus of our calls shifted from asking for business to "just checking on our clients, friends and family". With so much uncertainty in the economy we did not want to offend someone who may be worried about feeding their family by asking for business. We wanted to be encouraging and let them know that we are all going through this together. *"Spread joy to all who are discouraged. Encourage one another in the Lord." Isaiah 35:3-4*

One good thing about the pandemic was people were going to be confined to their homes, which meant they had time to take our calls. We reached out to everyone that we knew, past clients, friends, family without any business objective just checking on folks. This was a humbling experience, and well received. People were so elated that we just called to check on them many of them wanted to talk about business and even refer us business. Because of these calls, over the next couple of weeks, our business went through the roof, and we were selling houses like crazy.

When things were uncertain, and the country was in a panic, our team had a phenomenal month. April 2020, the first month of the pandemic we were blessed to sell over four million dollars of real estate; setting a record for monthly sales for my team. To put it in perspective, our team sold a little under 10 million during the entire year of 2019. This was a major accomplishment, and I could not be prouder of them. They each trusted the process and made it work. In addition to having a record month, something else great came out of this pandemic. I finally had the time to be still and fulfill my dream of writing this book. For the past two years, I have wanted to write a book but never could find the time. As a husband, father of two young boys, and a business owner, I am constantly adhering to a tight schedule. When the governor announced that everyone would be forced to stay home for six weeks, I figured it was now or never!

T. Mills

I am Terry. My professional identity to most is "T. Mills", the founder of T. Mills Realty Group. I am a realtor and recently started my journey as a real estate investor. Most importantly, I am the husband of Tiquela Williams Mills and proud father of our two wonderful boys, Trace and Tage Mills. Additionally, I serve as a deacon in my church, Mount Pilgrim Missionary Baptist in Fairfield, Alabama. My faith and my family are what motivate me to improve every day. However, in casually sharing my routine and marketing strategies with others, I have been told that I am a motivator and inspiration to those around me. That also encouraged me to write this book. I hope that reading my story will inspire you to take even your smallest dreams and transform them into huge successes. Like many of you reading this book, my roots are grounded in humble beginnings. Underneath the realtor, social media marketing coach, husband, and father, is a guy from a small middle-class area of Birmingham. I have lived most of my life in Alabama, but I was born in Boston, Massachusetts. Unlike most, my childhood mirrors the life of a military brat. However, my parents were never enlisted. I only lived in Boston until the end of first grade, but there are a few fond memories that I have from living there.

Bloodlines

My mother married my father, Edward, at the age of 20, and I was born soon after that. Unfortunately, an abusive relationship resulted in the end of their marriage when I was only a few months old. When I was ten months old, she met who would eventually become my stepfather, Jackie. I was so young when they married, he was the only father that I knew; therefore, I never looked at him as a stepfather. He was my dad. Because of how my biological father treated my mother, she never wanted me to have a relationship with him. However, Jackie felt differently. He felt that regardless of the strained relationship between my mother and Edward, I should still know my biological father. My mother eventually took my stepfather's advice and let me spend the weekend with my father when I was around seven or eight years old.

I vividly remember that weekend like it was yesterday. It was odd. We did not do any of the normal father and son things. I do not remember doing anything fun, like going to the park or playing basketball. I remember sitting in the house watching him drink most of the weekend. I also remember riding in the car with him as he made several random stops. At one stop, he left me sitting in the car alone for an hour in a dangerous neighborhood. I was scared to death.

When I got home, my mother asked me how the weekend was, and I lied. I told her we had a great time. I did not tell her what really happened because I figured she would not let me see him again. As fate would have it, that was the last time I saw him. A few months later, my mother received a call that my father was in the hospital with pneumonia. Several days later, we received another call that he died from bilateral pneumonia.

I did not know how to process the news. I was unsure if I should be sad or not because he was a stranger. Although I was so young, I felt that several pieces of his story were missing. I had no other memory to hold besides that one weekend we spent together and all of the weird things that happened. After his death, my mother never talked about my father. It was as if she was trying to hide something about him from me.

Southern Living

My family is originally from Alabama and I spent most of my summers as a child there with my grandmother. My mother, Deborah is the oldest of two girls. When my grandmother was giving birth to my mom's baby sister, my aunt Bridget, my grandfather left. With the responsibility of having to raise two children on her own my grandmother immediately sought work however, because this was during the Civil Rights Movement, she had difficulty finding work.

At the age of 20, my grandmother decided to move to New York where she was told there was a promise of stable work. Yet, she was faced with a very difficult decision of having to leave her children in Alabama with her mother. She found work in New York as a house sitter and soon met a new love and remarried. Not long after marrying she had another baby girl, my aunt Cecilia. When Cecilia was born she returned to

Alabama for my mom and aunt Bridget then moved to Boston in an attempt to give all of her daughters a better life.

The summer before second grade, my grandmother told me that I was going to live with her for a few months because my mom and stepdad were leaving Boston and relocating to Ohio. Even as a young boy, I remembered life being great while we lived in Boston, and I did not want to leave. We would frequently cook lobster and steak on the weekend and take summer vacations to Cape Cod. As a child, I thought this was normal. Now that I am older, I realize that we were quite fortunate to experience that lifestyle.

My stepfather was a construction worker, and job opportunities had begun to decline. In the fall of that year, they decided to move to Ohio so he could pursue a Commercial Driver's License for truck driving. My mother also enrolled in school to become an air traffic controller. I eventually joined them in the spring semester of second grade. Of course, I was looking forward to living with my parents again; but I was not looking forward to starting a new school. This would be my second school that year and third elementary school overall. The struggle was really real for a young kid. At first, things were looking good until my dad started applying for truck driving jobs.

While living in Boston, he was stabbed in the chest and had to have open heart surgery. Although he was relatively healthy, no company wanted to hire him because of his health risk. Since his aspiration of driving trucks was crushed, my family decided to move to Alabama, where we had more family support. We moved to Bessemer, an area about 20 minutes west of Birmingham.

Although we had the essentials, our life was nothing like it was in Boston. We no longer had lobster and steak nor family vacations. My father finally found a job driving cement trucks while my mother worked odd jobs like selling insurance, working in retail, and even in a chicken plant. My stepfather had a son from a previous marriage who started living with us as well. Although we never missed a meal and had a roof over our heads, this new Alabama life was tough.

I remember not being able to run the water while taking a shower because we were trying to conserve and save money. I could only run water just long enough to get wet, turn it off while lathering up, and turn it back on to rinse off. I can laugh about it now, but I remember my stepfather yelling, "TURN THAT WATER OFF!", if we attempted to shower longer than allowed. After a few years, my mother reached a breaking point that motivated her to go to nursing school. I remember this like it was yesterday. When she told my stepfather what she wanted to do, he told her it was a bad idea.

"We are barely making ends meet, and you want to spend money to go to school?" he said.

I am so glad that she stepped out on faith and pursued her plan because this was when our lives started to turn around. When my mother finally finished nursing school, we were so excited. It was such an inspiration for me to witness firsthand how hard she worked to accomplish this goal. After earning her nursing degree, she was faced with a new hurdle. Nobody was hiring nurses in Birmingham. After months of unsuccessful job searching, my parents decided to move to Atlanta, where she worked at the infamous Grady Hospital.

ATL

The Summer of 1996 the Olympics were in Atlanta. I was a rising 8th grade boy, so Atlanta was definitely the place to be. I remember thinking, this is going to be great! In addition to the Olympics, I had high hopes of seeing one of my favorite groups, Outkast. They were Atlanta natives and made the world see just how great the city was. Now I was living there, and for me, things could not be better. Living in Atlanta is what influenced me to dream big.

We moved to a city called Morrow, which was about 30 mins outside of the city of Atlanta. Morrow was a nice city, and this was the first time that I saw so many Black people doing well for themselves. I also started playing football. Life was good; however, things would soon change.

After several months, my mom's nursing career was taking off however, my stepfather was not so fortunate. The construction market in Atlanta was extremely competitive, and he could not keep a steady job. So, after a year, they made the hard decision to move back to Alabama. I was devastated. I loved my life in Atlanta, and I was not looking forward to leaving. While living in Atlanta, my parents kept our home in Bessemer, so we moved back into the same house that we lived in. I remember thinking to myself, we could have at least moved to a new neighborhood. A few years later, my parents purchased land in McCalla to build a house. McCalla was only 5 miles from Bessemer; however, the area was a tad bit newer.

    I felt like we were finally moving in the right direction. It took a couple of years, but during my senior year in high school, we moved into a beautiful 2500 square foot home. I did not realize it, but my parents' journey taught me a life lesson. Things will not always go as planned, and sometimes you will have to take a step back to move forward. However, all things are possible if you keep God first and work hard.

Mr. Tough Guy

Despite the lessons learned in patience and perseverance during my younger years, being forced to move around a lot had a negative impact on me, and I did not realize it until I became an adult. Moving from school to school adversely affected my ability to establish and maintain social relationships. After going to four different elementary schools, two middle schools, and a high school located on the other side of town, I never had a chance to form any real friendships. Sure, I was cool with several people, but by the time we would get to know each other well, we were moving again.

For example, my wife Tiquela has friends that she has been close with since preschool and elementary school. This is a beautiful thing, but because we moved so often during my childhood, I will never know what that feels like. Growing up, I was always the new guy, and because of that, I was forced to put on the tough guy persona. It was my defense mechanism because I did not know anyone, and I did not want to be tested. Yes, the tough guy persona earned a little respect. But it also gave me a reputation of being "stuck up" or acting as if I was better than others. The truth is, I just did not know how to interact with people, so to compensate for my insecurities, I would just stay to myself and never talk to anyone. It was not until I reached my 30's that I learned to put my guard down and just be nice to everyone. People see me now and think I am just a social guy, smiling on every picture and talking to everyone in the room.

Trust me I have not always been this comfortable in social settings. If it was not for high school football, I am not sure that I would have ever learned how to interact with others or developed any real friendships. Of course, I was cool with all of my teammates, but I did not have anyone that I could call a real friend until I met Will. Will and I met our freshman year. We both played the same position, defensive end, so we quickly developed a bond. Over the next few years, we continued to grow as friends and eventually considered ourselves as brothers.

Will was a good football player and an even better basketball player. After graduation,

Will received a scholarship to Lawson State, in Birmingham, and I attended the University of Alabama at Birmingham. So, we were able to remain good friends and hang out on the weekends. We still laugh to this day about how much time we spent at each other's schools. I would attend all of the parties at his school, and Will would attend all of the parties at mine.

During our freshman year in college, we were both required to stay on campus. The next year, we decided to get an apartment together and were roommates until we both finished college. We would eventually become godfathers to each other's children and best men in each other's weddings. Although Will and I had a great friendship, I still struggled with interacting with other people outside of my normal circle. One night I was out with Will and some of his friends, a totally new circle of people that I had not met. Since I did not know anyone, I was very uncomfortable, and socializing was just awkward for me. I just stayed in my own world and acted like I was enjoying myself. I eventually was approached by a guy that, in my opinion, dressed weirdly, and I figured had nothing in common with me. He proceeded to introduce himself,

"What's up man? I'm Freddy."

I kind of gave him a head nod and halfway shook his hand. Later on, I realized how wrong I was for treating Freddy like that. But at the time, I did not know any better. In hindsight, I realized just how much my transient living as a child impeded my socialization skills.

I was growing as a young adult but still did not understand how to engage with peers. Just recently, Freddy and I were reminiscing on the first time we met. He said, "Bro you were mean as hell." Freddy would ask Will, "What's up with Tuck?", which is what all of my friends call me. People would tell him, "He's cool... he just has to get to know you." Eventually, after I had gotten acquainted with people we would eventually become friends. That is just how I treated people that I did not know. I grew out of that phase and realized that all people are not out to hurt you, and it is ok to be nice. This lesson has been most beneficial in establishing my career in real estate. Tough guys are not approachable, and quiet guys cannot thrive in a realtor's world.

Truth Hurts

A few weeks before my high school graduation, I started thinking about my biological father. I began asking questions and wanted to know more about him. It just did not make sense to me for someone to die at a young age from pneumonia. My mother realized I was old enough to know the truth. She told me my father did die from bilateral pneumonia. However, it was because he was HIV positive. He was addicted to heroin and contracted the disease from a contaminated needle.

Although the news was hard to hear, I was not surprised. I started to reflect back on the weekend we spent together, and it all made sense. He was addicted to drugs, and I am sure when he left me in the car, he was in the dope house getting high. So, this was the real reason she did not want me around him. She also told me that he had two other kids that I had never met. I have a sister that is older than me and a younger brother. I could not believe the things that I was hearing and started to question why she was even attracted to him. She said he was a very nice man when they met, but he lived a risky lifestyle of hustling in the streets. He never really had a job but was always willing to hustle to make ends meet. She told me they met in a department store in Boston. She later found out he was not shopping in the store that day. He was actually boosting clothes, but he was a nice guy overall. However, when his drug addiction worsened, so did his personality.

    I never really told anyone that story for several reasons. Who wants to admit that their father was a junkie who died from AIDS? Although I kept it to myself, I did not deny it. I chose to use it as motivation. I never told my mother all of the details about our weekend together. I figured it was in the past and it should stay there. I promised myself that I would never fall victim to a controlled substance because I did not want to do what he did to me to my future children.

    The challenges my father succumbed to, in addition to not having the typical father/son relationship with him helped me grow into the man and father I am today. I learned at an incredibly young age that your DNA does not determine your future. God allowed time with my biological father for a reason, even if just for a short season, like that one weekend. Learning the truth about my biological father finally gave me that missing puzzle piece that I needed. No, it was not easy to hear, but it was necessary. I had no idea how many lessons would unfold from one person. However, I am grateful for them.

College Life

It was the last semester of my senior year in high school, and the only thing that people were talking about was going to college. There were endless conversations and decisions about what school they were attending and what would be their major. It was hard to believe that I was already at this phase in life. I remember the first day of my freshman year like it was yesterday, and I started asking myself, "Where did the time go?"

Regardless if I was ready or not, it was time to grow up and become an adult. Although I made good grades in high school, I was not sure if I would be successful in college. I did not have to try hard to pass most of my classes. If I made a "B" or a "C," I was happy, yet it would drive my mother crazy. I was good at charming girls to help me with my assignments, being a team captain of the football team and being voted most attractive in my senior class did not hurt either. However, none of that was going to matter in college. It was time to "man up" and start doing things on my own. The first thing that I had to figure out was what university I wanted to attend. I had finally narrowed it down to my top three choices. The University of Alabama at Birmingham (UAB) was only 30 minutes from where my parents lived. The University of Alabama, which is in Tuscaloosa, was also about 30 minutes from my parents' house. My other choice was Alabama State University, which is in Montgomery, Alabama, an hour away.

I decided to attend UAB for several reasons. One reason was it allowed me to remain in Birmingham to be close to my friends and family. My second reason was because my older cousin Jay, who I looked up to, not only attended but played football there. My third reason, which I guess should have been my number one, was it was a great school. Lastly, my mother really wanted me to go there, so she made a deal with me. She said If I went to UAB, she would pay for me to live on campus my first year. I immediately thought, "Bet!... That's a deal!".

I would have been a fool not to take advantage of her offer. I would have my own place on the Southside of Birmingham, which was not only home to UAB, but also one of the hot social spots of the city. That was a no-brainer for me. Once I broke the news to my friends, I do not know who was more excited. I am sure you have figured out by now my dorm room was the party spot every weekend. Aside from my social priorities, the next thing that I had to figure out was my major. What did I see myself doing for the rest of my life?

I did not have any male family members that attended college to talk to or ask for advice. Besides my cousin Jay who was attending UAB, I would be the first male to attend college in my generation. On the other hand, all of the women in our family were educated and making a great living for themselves. Most of them were either nurses or had other roles in the medical field, which was not appealing to me. I do not even like to go to the hospital when I am sick. I certainly did not see myself working in one.

My mother would ask me what I liked or what excited me, and my response was always the same. I wanted to own a business. I wanted to be my own boss. The problem was in school we were only told about the obvious careers; doctor, lawyer, nurse, or engineer. If I would have known that I could have my own business as a realtor, who knows where I would be now. Despite the lack of exposure and opportunities to explore various career options, I took her advice and decided to pursue pre-business.

It was near the end of the summer, and the hype from graduating high school was gone, the playing and vacation was over. It was time to get serious. Orientation was quickly approaching, and things were starting to become real for me. Freshman orientation was an opportunity to walk around campus to learn more about our class schedule and the university. While most of my friends were excited about starting college, I was extremely nervous. Like I stated earlier, high school was relatively easy for me. However, now that I would not have the teachers on my side and no friends to help me with my work, I was not sure if I could do it. Nevertheless, I kept my insecurities to myself and kept a smile on my face and pretended everything was "all good."

When orientation day arrived, my mother was extremely excited. She could not wait to get to the campus to see my dorm and find out what classes I would be taking. Once we arrived, the first thing that I noticed was none of the other kids seemed as nervous. Everyone else appeared to be confident and seemed to "have it all together." On the contrary, I was starting to question why I was even there. After studying my class schedule, I did not think I was smart enough to handle my courses. When I decided to declare business as my major, I did not consider what courses I would have to take. I was expecting classes on fun stuff like marketing and managing employees. I did not realize it would require accounting and several math courses. After realizing the courses I needed to graduate, I instantly felt defeated and was ready to go home.

Most people thought I was an extraordinarily strong and confident guy. The fact is, I was very insecure, and I still doubt my abilities even now. The difference between then and now is I am older and have learned to push through my fears. Through my experiences, I have grown to understand things are never as bad as they appear. For my mother's sake, I continued with the tour because I did not want to let her down. When we got home that afternoon, she could tell something was wrong. She came into my room to check on me.

She asked, "What's wrong, aren't you excited about starting college?".

As hard as it was to admit, I had to be honest and let her know that I was excited, but I also feared failing. I did not receive a scholarship, and college was not cheap. I just did not want to waste my parents' money or time. After we talked for a while, I finally got out of my feelings and decided to stick with it and give college a try.

A few weeks later was freshman move-in day. Now, this was exciting! I would have my own spot on campus, and the dorm was co-ed. All freshmen lived in Rast Hall, which was set up like apartments. There were two rooms on each side of the suite with a common area in the middle. I had three soccer players as roommates: Sam from Texas, TJ from Atlanta, and Matt, who was from Kentucky. We had a few days before class started, so we used that time to get to know each other. We sat around and discussed our goals and future plans after college.

I was amazed at how each of them had their whole life planned out, and I did not have a clue. However, I remained cool and played right along as if I had it all figured out. While listening to them discuss their plans to become engineers or lawyers, I reflected on the conversation that my mother and I had after orientation. She told me to just focus on me and not what everyone else is doing. If I went after my own dreams and did what made me happy, that was all that mattered. I realized that I was not like everyone else, and I was cool with that. No, I did not have it all figured out; but, I was determined to succeed. Just making it to college was something to be proud of, so I used that as motivation to keep going.

Classes started a few days later, and I was anxious. I was officially a college student. I was looking forward to starting class and meeting new people, mainly the girls. My confidence level was at an all-time high until I walked into my first accounting class. When I walked into the room, I could not believe my eyes. The classroom was the size of a movie theater and filled with hundreds of students. I felt defeated before the professor even started talking.

In high school, we would have several quizzes and tests throughout the year. However, college was different. We only had a midterm and a final. I felt as if I was immediately set up for failure. If I did not pass the midterm, I certainly was not going to pass the class. I ended up failing the midterm and dropping the class. I was now at a crossroads because in order to receive a degree in business, I had to pass accounting. I did not know what to do about my major.

The other disappointment was that college was just not fun for me. I was miserable and ready to quit. This was nothing like high school, where

I was one of the popular kids and knew everyone. At UAB, I was just another guy on campus. This was also the first time in years that I was not playing football, and it was killing me. I always dreamed of playing for UAB, just like my older cousin Jay. I thought maybe I should give it a try and walk on.

Looking back, football is what saved me and kept me focused in high school. If we missed class or made bad grades, we had to run. Nobody liked to run, so we did what we had to do to stay out of trouble. I needed that accountability and structure. I also missed the camaraderie and brotherhood that I had being a part of a team. I wanted to make lifelong friends in college. After talking it over with my parents, I decided to pursue college football.

During the spring semester of my freshman year, I decided to walk on to the football team, and my college experience instantly changed for the better. After working out and practicing with the team all winter, it was finally time for the Spring Game. The Spring Game gives coaches the opportunity to evaluate talent and fill positions for the Fall. Since I was just a freshman, I did not expect to get much playing time in that game, but to my surprise, I ended up playing quite a bit. I could attest to the old adage, "hard work pays off".

All my friends and family attended the game, and I felt as if I made them proud. However, I do not think anyone was prouder than my stepfather. At the end of the game, he came to the sideline, hugged me, and told me "good game." My mother said when they got home, he could not stop talking about it. He was even calling people and telling them I was going to the pros, although I did not see that happening. I am not sure why guys have a hard time showing emotions. With that said, it was good to know how my stepfather really felt.

After a successful return to football, I had also reached a decision about my major. Now that I was a college athlete, I was frequently around athletic trainers. After interacting with and observing them, it seemed like a really cool job; therefore, at the start of my junior year, I decided to change my major to sports medicine. Not only was this something that I really enjoyed, I did well in it.

However, after completing two semesters, my professor and I were discussing job opportunities in the field, and she dropped a bomb on me. "Athletic trainers work a lot of hours, but most do not make a lot of money unless you can make it to the college or professional level."

The wind was immediately removed from my ambitious sails. She did not want to discourage me; however, her honesty helped me realize this was not the path I needed to pursue. Here I was again, back at another challenging, life-changing crossroad. I had been in college for three years and still did not know what I was going to major in. At this particular point, most students are preparing to graduate within a year. The pressure of my timeline began to build. Most importantly, my parents added even more pressure by telling me they could only pay for one more year of college. After that, I would be responsible for all of my financial obligations. What was I going to do?

I planned a meeting with the athletic academic advisor to see what my options were. I explained that I needed a major that would only take about a year to complete. The two choices he gave me were education and criminal justice. I certainly did not see myself teaching, so I chose criminal justice. Now that I had my major figured out, I was forced to make another tough decision.

The NCAA would not allow college athletes to have a job. Even though I was an athlete, I was not on scholarship. I was a broke student athlete. While most players were on scholarships and received money for room and board, I was not and had to pay for everything out of pocket. Being on the football team was cool; however, being a broke college student was not. A few months later, I ended up leaving the football team to get a job. Although it was a tough decision, it was actually a smart move. I was able to get a job working in loss prevention at a department store. During my last two years in college, I worked full time hours during the day and took classes at night. Aside from being able to make money, working in loss prevention gave me the work experience that I needed to start my career.

After five years, I earned my Bachelor of Science in Criminal Justice. This was the beginning of my nine-year career as a probation officer.

The Probation Officer

I was entering the Spring semester of my senior year at UAB, and I still had no idea where I wanted to work. I just knew I wanted a job, and I wanted to do something big. I wanted a career that not only paid well, but one that would positively impact the world. There are only a few careers that you pursue with a degree in Criminal Justice. The choices were becoming a police officer, probation officer, lawyer, correctional officer, and working for the government. My top choice was to work for the Secret Service. I thought that would be the coolest job in the world. I imagined myself in sharp suits, dark shades, black cars, all while protecting the nation's leaders. It sounded like the perfect fit for me. Who would not want that job, right? If only it was that easy. I did not know anyone who worked for Secret Service, so my chances of securing a job like that were very slim. It is almost impossible to get in. My little criminal justice degree did not really hold any weight in comparison to the requirements for this job. Experience is the first qualification that the federal government looks for. You must have previous experience as a police officer, correctional officer, or other law enforcement role. Ironically, these were all jobs that I was not interested in. So now what? The only job left was to become a probation officer. At the time, I did not know much about the career. I asked one of my professors who once worked in the role to give me more information about the job.

After learning the details of the job, it seemed like something that would suit me perfectly. It was a desk job with a typical Monday-Friday schedule and paid a decent salary. Probation Officer it is! Now that I had decided on a career, the pressure was on to find a job. Lingering in the back of my mind was my mother telling me that she was giving me up to six months after graduation to assume responsibility for all my bills.

Until this point, I was unsure what I was going to do with my life, and I began to feel like a failure. I was in my 5th year in college, and my friends had either graduated or knew what career they were going in. Although I was at a crossroads in my life, I had become excited and could not wait until graduation. The first step was to submit my application and then take a written exam. After passing the written exam, I was invited to Montgomery to complete the endurance test. I was an athlete, and I was used to working out, so I was sure this would be easy. We were given physical capability tests that included running, pushups, sit-ups, jumping a fence, and other physical activities.

We were required to complete each station at a specific time to move on to the next one. At the beginning of the day, we started with around 50 applicants, but only 10 of us by the end. I was feeling encouraged. I started thinking to myself, "You got this! This is it! You are about to be a probation officer." Mentally I was already in the car, calling all my friends and family to tell them that I passed the endurance test, and all I had to do was wait for a call for an interview. Boy, was I wrong? The instructor walked into the room and informed us they would call us one by one for the interview. It was in the middle of summer, and we are all hot and sweaty and in gym clothes.

We were not prepared to be interviewed, but that was the point. They wanted to catch us off guard to test our ability to think when we were unprepared. The room was in total silence. Everyone was sat nervously, waiting for their name to be called. The door opened, and the interviewer announced, "Terry Mills you are next!"

I cannot remember the last time I was that nervous. I walked into the room, and a round table of 10 people were staring at me. I thought to myself, "Oh Lord, here we go!" If you have ever had a panel interview, you know that it is one of the world's scariest experiences. As I sat there sweating, I began to doubt myself. It was no way I was getting the job. I was mentally defeated before the interview even started. Questions started coming from right to left, and I just wanted it to end. When I returned home, I told my parents it was no way that I was going to get the job. Of course, they encouraged me to remain positive and wait until I heard back from the interview. A few weeks later, I received a letter in the mail informing me that I did not get the job. I was defeated and did not know what I was going to do. Everyone told me that it would take about six months after graduation to find a job, but I did not have six months. My mother had given me a timeline, and I would be responsible for paying my car note, insurance, and cell phone soon, so I had to find a job asap.

I was working loss prevention in the mall; my job was primarily catching shoplifters. It was a cool job. I walked around the store all day acting like I was shopping but I was truly looking for people who were attempting to steal merchandise. It was not a career, but it was definitely the catalyst. One Saturday night, my life changed forever. We caught a guy stealing jeans from the men's department. Once the police arrived, I pulled the officer to the side to introduce myself. I informed him that I had recently graduated from UAB with a criminal justice degree, and I wanted to be a probation officer. I explained that I previously applied with the state however, I did not get the job. I asked if he knew of any other companies that I could apply with. He gave me the number to call a guy that was over a private probation company. I was not familiar with the private sector however, I was willing to try anything.

I gave the guy a call, and he asked me to come in for an interview. I immediately got excited and started thanking God for answering my prayers. This is it! This is the job that I was praying for. I could not wait for the interview. All I kept telling myself was, "This is my job." I did not care about the salary or what the job consisted of. I just knew I wanted it. The interview came, and it was totally different from my previous experience when I applied with the state. It was just me and the supervisor. He was very laid back, and we had a casual discussion. He explained to me that he currently did not have an opening; however, something might be available soon, and he encouraged me to stay in touch. I remember calling him every week for at least a couple of months until finally, he told me to come back in for a second interview. When I went back for my second interview, it was not anything like the first one. This was a panel. I was thinking to myself why do probation officers require panel interviews? Either way, I was prepared this time, I just went in relaxed and did my thing. A few days later, I received a call that I had the job!

I used to joke and say that I am so thankful for the guy stealing that night because I never would have gotten the opportunity to meet the police officer that introduced me to the man that gave me my first real job. I guess the old saying is true, "A closed mouth doesn't get fed." This taught me a valuable lesson. Never be afraid to ask those around you for help. You never know who can connect you with the person that can create an opportunity for you. So here I was, Terry Mills, the probation officer! And just like everyone said, it took about six months for it all to come into fruition.

Who would have ever thought that I would become a probation officer? To this day, people still laugh when I tell them that I was a PO. The reality is, I really was not anything more than a glorified bill collector. Now, know that I am not minimizing the job because I would not be the businessman that I am today without that experience. Ironically, being a probation officer inspired me to want to own a business. The company that I worked for was private, which means we did not receive any funding from the city, state, or government. The people on probation paid a monthly supervision fee, which was the only funding that the company received.

For example: Let's say you had to come to court because you owed the city $1,000 in fines such as speeding tickets and had no insurance however, you did not have the money to pay them. The city would put you on probation to make payments instead of putting you in jail.

The company I worked for would put you on a monthly payment plan of $140 a month. $40 would go to our company, and $100 would go towards your fines. In 10 months, your fines should be paid off, and the company would have made $400 in supervision fees. Genius, right? It was a win/win for everyone. The defendant received time to pay their fines, the court received their money, and our company made profit.

This was a dream job for a kid fresh out of college. I had my own office, was on salary, and unlike many of my peers, I was actually using my degree.

I excelled fast in the company and had my own office within the first two years. Here I am, a college grad in my early 20's supervising people twice my age. I attribute my success as a PO to the fact that I was young, black, and relatable. The harsh reality was most of my defendants looked like me and were around the same age. As a result, they trusted me and were compliant with all instructions and advice I provided. I remember being out at clubs, and some of my defendants would be so excited that I was there that they would buy me drinks. Looking back, I do not think that was ethically correct. However, I just viewed it as an inexpensive way to say thank you.

My first management position was overseeing our Tuscaloosa office. Let me tell you this was definitely a learning experience. I experienced some things they do not teach you in college. One thing was how to deal with people. This was different from being in a probation office. Collecting money was easy; however, this was much more difficult. I was tasked with ensuring that my probation officers did their job, all policies and procedures were being followed, maintained a good relationship with our court staff, and most of all, the office was profitable. Although my first year was very challenging, it was my best year because the experience that I gained prepared me for the next opportunity.

I quickly learned the importance of not only performing and acting like a professional but dressing like one. Friday afternoon was our busiest time of the week. This was when most of our defendants would report to make payments on their fines. Although our office was large, we shared the parking lot with several other businesses in the area. From time to time, our defendants would occupy all of the parking spaces. Although our defendants would be in and out within 20 minutes, we would have an average of one hundred people reporting on a Friday, so it was constant traffic in and out of the parking lot. Eventually, one of the neighboring businesses got fed up and decided to go to City Hall to complain.

One Friday afternoon, we had a lobby filled with people. My staff and I were working very hard to get everyone in and out as fast as possible. Someone yelled from the lobby, "Hello!". I responded by saying, "Please sign in, and someone will assist you as soon as possible." Instead of responding, a man and a lady I had never seen before started walking toward my office. As a probation officer, I had to be tough and have a no-nonsense attitude at all times. Having two strange people ignore my request and walk back to my office did not sit well with me.

I proceeded to ask, "May I help you?".

The lady responded, "Yes, we are from the business licensing department with the city of Tuscaloosa, and we cannot find a record of this company's license. Please go get the manager so we can get this issue resolved.".

I proudly responded, "I am the manager." They both looked at each other with a look of disbelief. The man then asked to see the manager as if he was going to get a different answer.

Again, I proudly responded, "I am the manager."

He looked me up and down and asked, "You're the manager?"

I realized he was looking at my attire- jeans, sneakers, and a t-shirt.

He then said to me, "There's no way you are the person in charge."

I was standing there in front of my staff and a lobby full of our defendants. I immediately felt embarrassed and humiliated. Although the two city employees did not verbally say anything disrespectful, the look of utter disdain on their faces said enough. I knew that their initial glance of me did not earn their respect, and they were judging me simply because of my casual attire. I realized that day, the importance of dressing like a professional. You never know who is watching. No matter how educated, professional, and knowledgeable you are, in this world where people are judged by their looks, first impressions are truly everything.

While in a regional meeting the topic of growth and opportunity within the company was being discussed. I was excited to hear that our company had just landed the contract with the City of Birmingham, the largest account in the state. I thought to myself, "This is your job"! How cool would it be to run one of the largest offices in the company at the age of 25?

After the meeting, I told my supervisor that I wanted the job. Of course, he told me that I was not ready, and this was nothing like the current office that I supervised. The Birmingham office had many moving parts, and I would be responsible for 15 employees and a caseload of over 3,000 defendants. The City of Birmingham courthouse had multiple courtrooms, which meant I would have to establish a working rapport and appeal to various judges. I did not care. I wanted the job. I felt that I mastered running my current office, and I had become bored and felt stagnant. A few months went by, and I had not heard anything about the position. The Birmingham office was up and running, and I was making headlines within the company. As the young folks say, I decided to "shoot my shot" and ask him one more time if I could have the job. We went back and forth a few more weeks and finally he said, "If you want it, the job is yours."

I became the new manager for the Birmingham office. I was feeling like the sky was the limit. My salary drastically increased, but so did my responsibilities. This was a whole different world from my previous position in Tuscaloosa.

One of the main differences was the staff. In my previous office, I hired and trained everyone myself, so they were my team. However, this was his team. My biggest hurdle was getting them to trust and believe that I was the man for the job.

One of my first challenges was my age and earning the respect of employees that were old enough to be my parents. I was still in my twenties and everyone's initial thought was, "Who is this kid?". My next challenge was getting the judges to like me. We had a contract with the city, which meant they could fire us at any time, so the pressure was on. After a few months, the staff warmed up to me, so did the judges. Looking back at my career, this position was critical in preparing me for leadership. I could write a book alone just from some of the things I experienced in this role.

The company began to grow and we were managing cases in Alabama, Georgia, and Florida. I found myself getting bored again and wanted a new challenge. After reaching this position, there were limited opportunities for growth, but a few leadership positions opened in other parts of the state. Yet they did not spark my interest. So now what? I had been with the company for about four years and in my current position for two. I felt like

I had hit the ceiling and could not advance anymore.

Once again, I was at a point in my career where I felt discouraged and lost. To everyone around me, I appeared successful, but on the inside, I was frustrated and bored. There were not any other management positions available, and I was sure my supervisor was not leaving anytime soon. To my surprise, I was totally wrong! As you will find out later in the book he would end up getting fired and I would assume his role as probation director. By now I am sure you are saying to yourself; this is the luckiest guy in the world. To some extent, you are correct. It seems that I was always in the right place at the right time. However, a big part of it was seeing an opportunity and not being scared to take it.

I was Terry Mills, Probation Director for Central Alabama. Cool title, huh? My friends used to joke and say, "Boy, you are important now!" But basically, I was a regional manager. Instead of managing one office, I was now responsible for several offices across the state of Alabama and Mississippi. Instead of supervising probation officers, I was supervising their office managers. I spent most of my time on the road traveling across the state to visit offices to make sure my managers had everything they needed to be successful. I visited our courts to make sure they were satisfied with our services. Since all of our courts were contracts, it was now my responsibility to make sure the contracts were renewed every year. So, if that meant taking a judge to lunch or just visiting to talk, that's what I had to do.

On Mondays, I would drive to Mississippi, the next day I would be in Selma, the next day I would be in another part of the state. In addition to making sure our clients were happy, I was also responsible for growth. This was actually the fun part of the job. My new supervisor, who was the state manager, would give me a list of courts that the company wanted to add, and it was my job to do presentations to their city council explaining why they should hire us. This was the catalyst of my business ownership and management aspirations. I was running a business however, I was running someone else's business. My main job was to grow my area and make sure each office was profitable. This was the turning point in my life. I was now inspired to become an entrepreneur. It was time to stop running someone else's business and run my own.

Although the majority of my accounts were spread out across Alabama and Mississippi, my home office was still our Birmingham location.

When I was not traveling, I would spend most of my time in the Birmingham courthouse just to be the face of the company and make sure things were running smoothly. The Birmingham account was complex and very political, and because our CEO, Robert McMichael, would come to Birmingham whenever we had major issues or needed to get something done. Mr. McMichael was a well-respected man with an impressive resume. Prior to holding the position of CEO, he was a U.S. Marshall and the Sheriff of Dekalb County in Georgia. When he talked, people listened. Although he was the CEO and made all of the decisions, he was not familiar with the day to day operations in the Birmingham courts. Therefore, he would bring me along when he met with the judges and other city officials just in case, he was asked a question that he was unable to answer. I never really got the opportunity to speak in those meetings but being there taught me so much about business and how to handle myself in intense settings.

He who finds a wife

I was 27 years old, I had a great job, a nice apartment close to downtown, and made good money. Life was great. It was all good except for one thing I was ready to settle down. I really enjoyed the bachelor's lifestyle, but I was getting older. One of my biggest fears was being the 40-year-old man in the club trying to pick up women. Most of my boys were starting to settle down and have kids, so they were not as available to hang out as much. I lived it up during my early twenties, and I did not have any kids or responsibilities outside of work; therefore, I was free to do whatever I wanted. There I was with all this free time and nothing to do. I have never been a homebody, so staying in the house all weekend was not an option.

Birmingham had several night clubs and lounges; however, there were not many places for young professionals. The club crowd was either too old or too young. Since I was underwhelmed with the nightlife, I decided to take my talents to Atlanta. The short two-hour drive made getting off work on Fridays and riding down I-20 a simple task. The nightlife scene was much different than I was accustomed to at home; it was a single man's playground. One of my favorite spots to go to in Atlanta on Saturdays was ESPN Zone, a sports bar located downtown. Most weekends, it was filled with young professionals watching the games, laughing, and having a good time.

Although I enjoyed hanging out at the sports bar, I really went to Atlanta for the nightlife. Atlanta was known for having some of the best strip clubs; my favorite spot was the infamous Magic City. The strip club scene is not what most people think it is. Yes, of course, they have dancers; however, many come to enjoy the music, drinks, and the chill vibe. I was a little shy when I first started going, but after a few visits, I found my groove. I was so good that I even started dating one of the girls that worked there. It was something new and exciting. I mean, let's be honest, how many men could say that their girl worked at Magic City? She lived in Atlanta, and I lived in Birmingham; therefore, I did not have any relationship expectations. I did not see it going anywhere, and I was just having fun. For about six months, we took turns driving to each other's city. Eventually, I got tired of going back and forth to Atlanta, plus outside of hanging out and having fun, we realized that we were not compatible.

Until that point, I had fun dating and hanging out with different women. However, no one really sparked my interest. Most women I dated were either having too much fun, did not have any plans for their future, or were too focused on their future and did not know how to have fun. I was looking for someone like me. A woman that was cool, down to earth but could handle business when it was time to. For a while, it did not seem like this woman existed until one day, I was over my friends Antjuan's house. Antjuan was a good friend of mine that was also living a bachelor lifestyle similar to mine. We would usually be at his home, either barbequing or watching sports, and he was also my wingman during my Magic City days in Atlanta.

Antjuan had another good friend named Ashley. Ashley and Antjuan were like brother and sister, and they hung out a lot. Most of the time, when I came around, Ashley was there as well. I really liked Ashley; although she was a girl, we treated her like one of the guys. Ashley was smart, cool, laid back, and liked to have fun. Just the type of woman that I was looking for. One day we were all over Antjuan's house, and I asked her, did she have any single friends. She replied no one that you would be interested in you; however, I do have an older sister Tiquela. Instantly she had my attention.

I was intrigued. Yet Ashley informed me that her sister would not be interested in me. She said she was looking for someone serious and not interested in playing games. Although I tried to convince her that I was serious and ready to settle down, Ashley did not believe me because she knew about the wild stuff me and Antjuan did. After all, she was always around us. After asking her several times to tell me more about her sister, she finally gave in.

"She is older than you." She replied, annoyed.

"I like older women," I replied slyly.

"She is a nurse."

"My mother and grandmother are nurses."

"She is a Delta."

"SOLD!" I replied.

Ever since college, I had a thing for the women of Delta Sigma Theta Sorority, Inc. They were always super cool and fun to be around. I was ready to meet her. Although I had not seen her from the things that Ashley told me, I was interested. Antjuan was throwing a party in the next few weeks, so I asked Ashley to invite her sister. Ashley still did not take me seriously; however, she said that she would.

While parking my car on the day of the party, I noticed that I parked right next to Ashley and her sister Tiquela. I got out of the car, but I did not speak; I let them go ahead of me. After a while, I noticed her from across the room. I liked what I saw and thought that I would like to meet her. I could tell that she was also watching me from across the room. Finally, I walked to her and handed her my phone, then I asked her to put her number in my phone. After she finished, I took my phone back and walked away. During the party, we caught each other's eye a couple of times, but we never talked. I made sure that I could see her throughout that night to feel what she was like. I wanted to know was she comfortable kicking it, and did she like to hang, or if she was stuck up. I liked what I saw. She was lovely, she had her legs out, and she was looking sweet. When I got home that night, I texted her to see if she made it home safely (really to see if she gave me the right number). I was relieved when she replied to let me know that she was home. I did not want to seem anxious, so I told her I would call her the next day. The next day which was Sunday, I called, and we talked forever. Before the end of the conversation, I told her she was going to be my girl.

She did not have any kids, she was laid back, hard-working, she had her own crib and her own money. I did not feel pressured as I had with other women, who pressed the issue to get married or thought that we were a couple after one date. My mother told me that when I found the right one, I would know it.

For our first date, I invited her over for Monday Night Football. I was surprised that she knew more about football than any other woman that I had met. After that night, I could not wait to see her again, but I did not want her to know that. On the second date, we sealed the deal and began seeing each other regularly. Although we were dating, I was still seeing other people, and she knew. We were not in a committed relationship; we were just two people enjoying each other's company. I found myself talking with her about situations with other women, and she gave me her opinion. In some instances, she took my side. How cool is that? We continued to date over the next few months, and the other female friends in my life were falling by the wayside, and I was spending more time with her. One night while on the phone we had a bad argument, I cannot remember what it was about now, so I hung up thinking that was the end. I was disturbed, but I did not know what else to say. Ten minutes later, she was knocking at the door. I thought to myself, did she just pop-up on me? This was not her usual behavior, but I let her in, and we continued to argue about something stupid. The argument ended with both of us, admitting that we really wanted to be together. The next few months were great. We started traveling, partying, and just hanging. One night after attending Antjuan's Christmas party, I arrived home to find that my place had been burglarized. I called Antjuan, and he and Ashley came over. I was furious because the place was a mess, and I could not lock the front door. Ashley could see how upset I was and asked if I wanted to stay at her Tiquela's place for the night.

Tiquela worked night shift as a nurse, and she was at work when I discovered I was robbed. I accepted Ashley's offer, and she gave me a key. The next morning when Tiquela got home from work, she came home to find me in her bed. I was so upset the night before that I did not think to call and tell her what happened. Tiquela was cool with me being there and told me to take as much time as I needed to find a new spot. That was one thing that I really liked about her; she was always patient with me and drama free. A few weeks went by, and everything was cool living together, but I decided to let the old apartment go. I had never lived with a woman, but I was enjoying our time together. I did not have anywhere to stay, and I could not afford where I wanted to live. Of course, my mom said that I could move back home, but that was not an option. I had not lived with my parents since High School.

A few months later, I was still living in her apartment. One day I came home from work, and Tiquela was in the kitchen cooking. I went off for no reason. I accused her of trying to trap me. Things felt too perfect, and I had never experienced that before. The old me began to creep back in.

"Are you crazy? I'm just cooking!" she yelled.

The argument continued, and she finally said, "You can go and find you an apartment!"

I was shocked and torn. I did have a desire to get my own place, but I did enjoy living with her. I was shocked that she was willing to let me leave, but my ego would not let her know that.

So I replied, "Yeah! Maybe I should get my own place!"

The next week we went looking for an apartment for me together. I saw a couple of places that I liked, but they were more than I could afford. I did not want to settle, and she could tell. She told me that I did not have to rush to find a place. Now I was wondering did she want me to go because I really did not want to? I was cool with our new lifestyle, and we really enjoyed each other. I decided to live with her for a few more months.

One of the things that we really enjoyed was traveling together. Every trip was fun and memorable. However, during one trip to Atlanta, the dynamic of our relationship changed. It was the BET Hip Hop Awards Weekend, one of the most star-studded weekends in Atlanta. I attended before, but Tiquela had not, so I was trying to impress her.

I reserved a room at the Intercontinental Hotel, where many celebrities stayed, and there was plenty of action. We pulled my 2-seater hardtop convertible Benz SL500 into the front of the hotel looking fly! I pulled up to the valet with the top down, had my lady with me, and everything was good. When we entered the lobby, the first person we saw was NeNe Leaks from the Housewives in the lobby, and Tiquela was a big fan of the show. As we proceeded to the front desk to check-in, I heard people screaming. I turned around, and it was none other than Floyd Mayweather and his entourage. Floyd's party was about 50 people deep. I thought to myself that it was going to be a great weekend. When I glanced at her, she had one of the biggest grins I had ever seen on her face. I was feeling like the man. We finished checking in, and when we walked to the elevator, we ran into Diddy. Tiquela is a big Diddy fan, and she wanted to take a picture with but was too afraid to ask. She ran out to follow him, but she was unable to catch him. She was super excited and impressed with the weekend thus far.

Later that night went to a club where the rapper TI was hosting the party. Leaving the party, we got into the car, and my car would not shift into drive. After a few attempts, the car cooperated, and we made it back to our hotel. The next day as we headed to Lenox Mall to go shopping, I noticed that my car was still in the same spot from the night before. The valet usually leaves the expensive cars in front to attract customers. I was thought to myself, "Oh, they must like my car."

I approached the valet attendant and asked for the keys.

He replied, "Oh, this is your car? We couldn't get it out of park last night. We need for you to move it."

Tiquela looked at me, confused, and I tried to play it off as if it was not a big deal. My attempts were unsuccessful, and I was unable to get it into gear. The valet was backed up, people are blowing and cursing at me to get my car out of the way. I was so embarrassed. Tiquela was looking at me, but I was trying to be cool. I was unsure how much it would cost to get my car repaired, and honestly, I did not have the money to pay for it. The hotel began to pressure me about moving the car. I had no choice but to have it towed to a local dealership to have it checked out. Because it was a weekend, the service department was closed, so they would not be able to look at it until Monday.

We had to stay an extra night, and I still did not know how much the repairs would cost.

The weekend was ruined. I still tried to enjoy the trip, but Tiquela could sense I was worried about my car. Monday morning, I received a call from the dealership explaining how much the repairs would cost. Talk about sticker shock! I did not have the money to fix it nor enough to stay three days while it was being fixed. Just two days ago, I was feeling like the man, and now I was embarrassed because I did not have enough money to get us back home. I had to swallow my pride and explain to Tiquela my situation.

She immediately responded, "Don't stress, I got you!"

I had never been the type of guy to ask for help, so I was utterly shocked by her response. She really made me feel ok about everything that happened. I called my mother to pick us up.

Mom got a big laugh from the situation. "You're over there trying to impress people and can't get your car running." Of course, Mom still came and picked us up, but everybody laughed about it on the way back to Birmingham. That is everybody but me.

The weekend led to a reflection on our relationship. I realized that Tiquela really had my back. She was not with me for the fun, flash, and good times; she was with me through the good, bad and the ugly. I never had a female that I could call a true friend. I have plenty of associates but nobody that I could really trust like her. Things were getting serious, very serious. I began asking myself, "Is this the woman that I wanted to spend the rest of my life with?" I was at a point in my life where I was super focused on my career. It seemed like the only thing that was missing in my life was a family.

Tiquela was super modest and responsible. There were things that she wanted but would not pursue. I was just the opposite. I would spend money freely. She always wanted a BMW650 but did not want to go for it. It was not that she needed a car because what she was driving was paid for. After searching online, we found one that she really loved. We went to the dealership, and she loved the car, but she was still hesitant. The car was midnight blue, tan leather interior, M Sports package, paddle shifters; it was fully loaded. This was her car. She really loved the car but was nervous about buying it. I told her, "Get the car, I've got you." Reluctantly she agreed and purchased the car, and this was a big deal for her. She had never let her guard down and depended on me. Although we were living together, we had separate accounts. This was a big step for her to trust me and lean on me for a change. This was a milestone in our relationship. I knew she was the one I wanted to spend the rest of my life with, and this was her way of showing me that she wanted the same. As we drove to pick up the car, I began to think, "Why am I waiting?" We talked about marriage over the past couple of months, and we even picked out a ring. The next day I went to the jeweler and bought the ring. When I left I called my best friend Will and asked him to come over, I was nervous. Will has been my best friend since high school, and I wanted him to be a part of this. Then I called Tiquela's sister Ashley and told her what I planned to do. She introduced us, so she had to be here too.

When I got to the house, Ashley and Will were waiting for me, and Tiquela was about 30 minutes away. I was so nervous I began pacing back and forth. Will asked, "Man are you alright?" I was retiring, this was my last dance, I was getting out of the game, hanging up my player jersey! When she finally got home, she immediately calls the insurance company and stays on the phone for what seems like forever. She was so excited about the new car; she did not see this proposal coming. She was going to remember this day forever!

When she got off the phone, I stood up and thanked Ashley for introducing us and treating me like family. Then I got down on my knee and asked Tiquela to marry me. She was in such shock she kept laughing. It felt like I was down there for two to three minutes. I thought she better say yes. After what seemed like forever, she finally said yes! We hugged and cried, then she started calling her family to tell them the good news. I was feeling pretty good. She had just purchased her dream car, we were getting married, and everything was great. A couple of days later, Tiquela said we needed to talk. I was nervous because I had no idea what she wanted to talk about.

"My dad is upset because you didn't ask him for his blessing before you proposed." She informed me.

I was shocked. It never crossed my mind to ask him. I honestly did not think that was something that people still did. I realized that I needed to apologize to her father if he felt offended. I had to honor that relationship and do things correctly. I met him the next day, and we sat down and talked. When we met, I was nervous. I told him that I did not mean to disrespect him. It just never crossed my mind to ask him first.

He asked me a few personal questions, and within five minutes, he said he gave his blessing, and we began discussing sports.

Six months later, we were married.

We went into our marriage as a partnership. I am the CEO, and she is the CFO. My job is to make sure that I create opportunities that enrich our lives and be the household's head. As the CFO, her role is to keep us from overspending and making sound financial decisions. I promised to be the provider, and that promise to her is what drives me every day. Being more of a risk-taker and Tiquela's more grounded, we balance each aspect of our lives. Eight years and two kids later, I have not fallen short on my word!

Business Goals

Deciding to open my own business was easy. The challenge was determining the type of business and the amount of work it would take to successfully start and maintain it. My top two choices were becoming a barber or opening a sports bar. Although these are both great businesses to own, they were not for me. I considered barbering until I actually spoke to my barber about my idea. My barber and I have a great relationship and talk often. We even worked out together for a few years. During our workouts, we would talk about business, and he expressed the frustrations he experienced as a barber. He worked every weekend and was on his feet eight to ten hours a day. I never took those things into consideration. I guess because I am only there a few hours out of the month. I also did not view barbers as business owners however, I was sadly mistaken. He was responsible for his own marketing, ordering supplies, profit of the shop, and customer service. Although barbers earn a great living, this was not the best fit for me.

What about opening a sports bar? The thought sounded great! Who would not want to have the best sports bar in the city? We are in the South, where sports serve as a common thread among all. Birmingham is a buzzing hub, especially during football season. Football in the state of Alabama is almost as big as politics, so owning a sports bar sounded like a great idea. I could see it clear as day! My spot would be full of people cheering for their favorite team on Saturdays. I even came up with the name, "The 5th Quarter". Get it? There are four quarters in a football game, and my bar is where people would come hang out once the game was over. It has a nice ring, doesn't it?

I had it all mapped out from menu choices to the interior and exterior color schemes. If it was not for my job at Shoney's, I probably would have pursued this dream. Yes, I worked at Shoney's when I was in high school. It was my first real job at age 16. Like most kids, I could not wait to get a job so I could have my own money. I wanted to experience not having to ask my Mom and Dad for anything. It was the summer before my junior year, and I was determined to work anywhere. I just wanted to get out of the house to make some money.

After applying across the city with different establishments, Shoney's was the first to hire me. You will never guess what position they hired me for a cook. I thought, "Wait...who? Me?". I took the job. Needless to say, it was hard. Working in the kitchen was really tough because I not only had to learn all of the meals, but each meal was cooked to order. If a customer wanted a steak cooked medium and I cooked it well done, guess what? It was coming back to the kitchen, and that meant the server would be upset because that usually effected their tip. Outside of the stress of the kitchen, the restaurant business was long hours. Closing at 10 pm did not mean I got off at that time. I remember one Saturday night, a bus full of people pulled into the parking lot at 9:45 pm with about 20 people on it. All of the staff looked at each other saying, "Are you serious?"

The customers ordered everything from steak to fish and chips. Even though I had already started cleaning and putting everything away for the next day, I had to do it all over again. The customers had left Tuscaloosa watching the Alabama Crimson Tide play. It was common to have Alabama fans stop there because Bessemer was the next largest city after leaving Tuscaloosa. I just wish they had not stopped that night because I was tired and ready to get home. It appeared that some of them had a few too many drinks because they were very loud and rude.

After they received their food, several of them sent their plates back to the kitchen, complaining that their order was wrong. Tension was high between the guests and the entire staff, and we could not wait for them to leave. They finally left around 2:00 am, and we still had to stay and clean up. Let's just say that was the day I reached the conclusion that food service was not for me.

So, now what? What business could I start that would not require a large amount of money and be something that I would enjoy? I started to search the internet for ideas and found an ad for a franchise opportunity with a janitorial service. Boom! This was it. No, it was not a business that was as sexy as a sports bar, but it did not require a lot of capital to start. I could do the work during the night and go to my full-time job during the day.

As probation director, I was responsible for paying all of the invoices to the janitorial company that cleaned the offices in my region.

Not to discredit them, but they would only spend about 30 minutes cleaning each office one day a week despite the amount of money we were paying them. Before seeing the ad, I had not viewed them as a business. I just saw a husband and wife cleaning our offices once a week. Boy, was I wrong.

By now, I had been with the company for a few years and had developed a good relationship with the couple. I could not wait until the next time I saw them to ask them more about their business. The next time the couple came into the Birmingham office it was business as usual. The wife began vacuuming while the husband emptied all of the trash. When the husband entered my office, I asked if he had a minute to talk. He responded, "Sure, what's up?". I informed him that I was considering starting a janitorial service and wanted to know more about the business. He explained that he and his wife had been in business for about ten years, and they loved it. The work was hard; however, it did not require a lot of time, and the money was very good. He said they had several large accounts that they serviced which brought in about 10k a month. Wow! I thought to myself, here I am in a nice corner office with a suit on, and he is here emptying trash in jeans and t-shirt and making twice my salary. Never judge a book by its cover.

I went home that evening and told my wife about the conversation I had that day with the couple. She could not believe it! We both prayed about it and did a little more research. Then we decided to step out on faith and give it a try.

We finally scheduled an appointment with the janitorial company that I found online to learn more about the franchise opportunity. We did not know what to expect, but we were very excited to learn more about the opportunity. The meeting took place later that same week in their office. My wife and I arrived in business suits ready to learn. When the manager came to the lobby to get us, she looked at us with a peculiar smirk as if she wanted to ask, "Who do you all think you are?".

Apparently, we were overdressed for this profession. This was a business opportunity, and that is how we approached it. The lady was very nice and professional. She gave us an overview of the company and explained how the franchise model worked. It was a very cool concept. They offered different packages that required the franchisee to invest a certain amount. In return, the company would guarantee a certain amount of business each month. For example, we purchased a $10,000 package and they guaranteed at least $3,000 a month in business. An extra $3,000 a month sounded good to us! However, we did not have the $10,000 to invest. Luckily the company had an option where we could invest a percentage of the $10,000 and finance the rest. That was the only option for us, and we decided to go for it.

We quickly signed the franchise agreement and felt like our power couple dream was coming true! I remember leaving that office feeling like I was on top of the world. Not because it was my dream to own a janitorial company, but because we were finally starting our own business.

Instead of heading straight home, we decided to go out to dinner to celebrate. This was an exciting time, and I wanted to enjoy the moment. At dinner, we laughed and talked about the many opportunities this could open for us. Who knew how big this could be? Outside of the guaranteed business the company would offer, we had the opportunity to get our own accounts as well.

We did not have any kids, so we could dedicate all of our time to working our full-time jobs and growing our business. The first thing we had to do was create an LLC to protect us. In order to do that, we had to create a company name.

Surprisingly, this was the hardest part of the whole process. What would our name be? After a couple of days, we agreed on a name, TM Corporate Services.

Now that our company had an official name, we needed a logo and business cards. This was exciting! I had business cards with my full-time job. However, it was nothing like seeing my name on our own business cards. I remember staying up late, playing on the internet, trying to come up with ideas. This was so important to me, and I could not focus on anything else. I was determined to make this company successful.

My plan was to take everything that I learned as a Probation Director and apply it to this business. Everything that I do, I want to do it big. My plan was to become the biggest franchisee that the company had in Birmingham. Before we could receive any accounts, we had to complete the training course. We learned how to do everything from cleaning windows to buffing floors. I did not think cleaning a building took that much skill. I was sadly mistaken. Every task had to be executed meticulously. One mistake in mixing chemicals would completely destroy a tile floor.

Once we completed training, it was time for us to get to work. One of our very first accounts was a small school. We cleaned it every day between the hours of 6:00 pm and 6:00 am. The next account was a clinic that only had to be cleaned twice a week during the same hours. Before I knew it, we had several accounts, and business was growing. As an ambitious person, every time the company was offered a new account, I accepted it. It did not matter how big the account or how many days a week it had to be serviced. I wanted it. I was hungry and was determined to be successful. On the other hand, my wife is a little more cautious and reserved. And if I am being totally honest, much smarter. That is why we are a perfect balance.

She would constantly tell me to slow down. We did not have any employees. That left us with the daunting task of cleaning every single building. She worked at UAB Hospital as a nurse in the Cardiovascular/Thoracic OR. As you can imagine, this was a very demanding job. I was still working my full-time job in probation services. However, my schedule was not as demanding. I had many responsibilities, but I could work from home. Since I did not have to report to an office every morning, I did not mind staying up late at night cleaning buildings.

After a while, we had too many accounts for me to service at night, so I decided to clean them early in the morning. For two years, I would wake up at 2 am to head to my first building and would not finish my last building until around 6 am. Once I finished, I would return home to get ready for my day job. The grind was real! The first building on my route was a small engineering firm, about 15 minutes from my house. This account was easy as the building was only about 2,000 square feet. Thankfully, it did not take me very long to clean. I only had to vacuum, empty trash, and clean the bathrooms. My next stop was a clinic. It had only been open a few months, and everything was like new. That made this account easy to clean as well. Now, my third stop was a much larger clinic. This account required much more attention. Although my duties were the same, the building was much larger. Therefore, it took a little more time to clean. The biggest challenge? Cleaning a large building in the middle of the night by yourself. Needless to say, I stopped watching horror movies.

During those two years, we serviced an average of seven to ten different accounts. At times the work was overwhelming. Getting up every morning at 2 am rain, shine, sleet, or snow, making sure each building was cleaned before opening was challenging. I understand "to whom much is given much is required" so I did not mind working hard. However, the hardest part of this business was keeping the clients happy. At the end of each month, the company that we bought our franchise from would send out review forms to all of our accounts, asking for feedback. This was the part of the business that I was not prepared for. I quickly learned the importance of customer service.

For example, we had a nice small church that we cleaned for over a year. The office manager and I had a great relationship; therefore, we would always get great reviews. It only took one person to make that change. One day I arrived to clean and noticed that the person that I previously reported to no longer worked there. They had hired a new office manager. This person and I never established a great relationship. At the end of that month, we received our first bad review for this account.

For over a year, we received nothing but great reviews, yet due to the lack of relationship with the office manager, things were different. We eventually lost that account due to the client not being satisfied with the work. I wish that I could say that would be the only account that we would lose, but it was not. After two years, instead of growing, our business was starting to decline. This was partly due to burnout. Remember when my wife told me to slow down and don't grow too fast? She was right.

Although the money was good, I was tired and frustrated. The schedule that I initially worked was no longer sustainable. Imagine getting up every morning at 2 am, working two jobs, and still trying to have a social life. It just was not possible. I remember going out with our friends on the weekend and having to leave early because I had buildings to clean. That sucked! In addition, the stress of pleasing difficult customers began to weigh heavily. No matter the quality of work performed, some people were just never satisfied. Eventually, my wife and I walked away from the business. It just was not worth the stress. Once again, I felt like I had hit a ceiling. This time it was with my own business. I remember lying in bed shortly after asking myself, "where did I go wrong?". I did not lack desire, ambition, or the drive to be a successful business owner. So, what was it? Then it hit me. I did not have a plan.

I was only focused on making money and making it quick. I should have taken the time to write out a business plan. I was just working. Instead of managing the business, I was too consumed with doing all of the work. My biggest mistake was not hiring any help. Instead of hiring employees to do the work, I was the employee. Every time we received a new account, there was more money, but that also meant I would have more work to squeeze into my schedule. In addition to that, anytime we would receive a complaint, I would have to personally fix the problem. Not to be misled this was not a bad experience. It was just the catalyst for developing into a business owner and learning valuable lessons. The things that I learned during those two years would only prepare me for the next business venture Real Estate.

Reality Checks

Almost everyone that I know has either tried or thought about pursuing real estate. So why not me? I mean, if they could do it, I am sure I could, right? There were so many things about the field that were attractive to me. I could wear nice suits, drive a fancy car, have my picture on signs all over the city, and make a lot of money. It was a no brainer. Although there is some truth to that perception, I soon found out being successful in real estate would take a lot of work as well. I was still working as Probation Director, so just like our cleaning business, this would require me to work in the evening and on the weekends. However, I was ready for it. I did not see any opportunity for advancement at my current job, and my cleaning business was failing. What did I have to lose?

At first, I wanted to be a real estate investor and flip houses. I would hear about how much money people were making and how easy it was. The concept was pretty simple. Buy a house for a cheap price, renovate it, and sell it for a profit. Sounds easy, right? Well, the concept is simple; however, the process is not. Therefore, I decided to sign up for one of those online training classes to learn more. The course was designed to teach me everything from branding to how to find private money.

Every week, I was glued to my computer for hours at a time, determined to learn as much as I could about flipping houses. Just the thought of me being a real estate investor kept me motivated to finish the course. After about six weeks, I still did not feel like I knew much about this business. I was learning but not enough to jump out into the field and get started. I needed real life interaction and some field training. I decided to reach out to some people that I admired as professionals to get some advice or at least point me in the right direction.

After talking with several people, the conversation that impacted me the most was with Kevin Howard, a successful attorney in Birmingham, but most importantly, he is a cool, down to earth guy who would eventually guide me in the right direction. During our meeting, I expressed my desire to pursue real estate and flip houses. I told him that although I was taking an online course to learn about the industry, I still had questions about the business. After talking for about 30 minutes, he stopped and asked a question that would change my life.

"T, why won't you be a realtor first because you don't know anything about real estate."

Although this was a simple question, it was one that changed my life. He was right. I did not know anything about real estate and becoming a realtor could teach me the business. As I sat there for a minute, I could not help but think about our failing cleaning business. I had to be honest with myself and admit that it failed because I did not properly prepare. I was so busy trying to grow instead of taking the time to learn more about the business. I could not afford to make the same mistake twice, so I decided to take his advice. I did not leave with the information I was seeking, I did leave with clarity.

Kevin gave me the contact information for a friend of his named Gabriel, a successful realtor who could tell me more about the business. It was funny that she was the person he connected me with because I constantly saw her signs all over the city, and I would say to myself, "she is really successful." After reaching out to her, I was blown away with the information I received. Outside of the endless opportunity for growth and income potential, I would be able to market and brand myself as well.

I was super excited and ready to become a realtor. I remember telling all of my friends and family what I was about to do. Unlike when we started the janitorial business, several people were excited and told me they could see me selling real estate. I was admired for running the janitorial service, but cleaning toilets and emptying trash was not as exciting as giving someone the keys to a new home. I remember sitting outside in my garage, talking to my brother-in-law one evening. I mentioned to him what I was about to do.

"Bro, you have what it takes to be successful in that field. Just take the managerial skills you learned from your day job and the hard work and discipline from your janitorial job, and you can't lose."

He also told me that he and my sister in law would be my first clients. Now, it was time to get to work. The first step was completing the 60-hour real estate course, so I looked online to see what was available. I found a Groupon for a course that was only $200. Yes! This is it. The class would start the first week of January 2015. It was a four-month course held two nights a week from 6 pm-10 pm. Let me remind you, I still had my day job and the janitorial service, so this was going to be a crazy schedule. I would still have to wake up at 2 am, clean my buildings, go to my day job until 5 pm, and then go to class at 6 pm. This was going to be tough; however, I was determined to get it done.

Big risk, big reward, right? Honestly speaking, I did not think the course was going to be that hard. I was just going to be selling houses. How much could there be to learn? Prior to taking the class, I did not know what the full-time duties of being a realtor entailed. I thought I would just show up to work with a list of people on my desk that needed to buy a house. Why did I need a 60-hour course to teach me that? I realized how wrong I was and was in for a rude awakening.

The first night of class came, and I could not wait to get started. I remember waking up that morning feeling like a child on Christmas waiting to see what Santa Claus had for me under the tree. When I arrived at class that evening, I took a picture of the book and posted it on Facebook with the hashtag, #realtorinthemaking. From day one, I started marketing myself. There was not a doubt in my mind that I would not finish the course. The instructor introduced himself and started off by telling us that most people do not finish the course, and those that do will probably not pass the state test the first try. What?? Are you serious? There I was thinking this was going to be a cakewalk. That is when my insecurities and self-doubt began sabotaging my thoughts. I already told the whole world I was about to become a realtor, so there was no turning back.

As we started to go over the class outline, I noticed that the course did not really talk about houses at all. We were going to learn about easements, state law, math, and a bunch of other stuff that I was totally not interested in. Although this was going to be harder than I thought, I stuck with it. After about four weeks, the excitement had worn off, and I was getting exhausted. Between working two jobs and trying to study, I was over it and ready to finish the course. Of course, I kept going and made it to the end. Now, it was finally test time.

First, we had to pass the class test with an 85 before we could sit for the state test. There was no way I could pass this test without studying, so I decided to take a few days off from work to get prepared. Trying to retain all of the information that we learned was very hard. Most nights, I was fighting to stay awake in class from lack of sleep. Either way, my excuses were not going to get me an 85, so I had to pass. When I got to class that night, I remember looking around the room at my classmates. It looked like we were at a funeral. Everyone looked sad and nervous because none of us knew what to expect. I was relieved knowing that I was not the only one worried about passing. After answering a few questions, I realized that it was not that bad. There were only a few questions that I did not know, but overall, I felt pretty confident that I would pass, and guess what? I did!!

Now that the class test was out of the way, it was time for the state test. I kept hearing that it was hard and to get prepared to take it more than once. Being the overachiever that I am, I was determined to prove everyone wrong and pass it on the first time. Because it was so much material, I gave myself two weeks to study in hopes that I could pass it on the first try. Nothing else mattered more than passing that test. It was the last hurdle that I would have to cross before I could become a realtor. I began posting every week on social media that I was about to become a realtor. I was already picking up potential clients, so this had to happen. When I arrived at the test center, I noticed one of my classmates sitting in the lobby. Seeing him there immediately calmed my nerves. It was good to see a familiar face. When I approached him, he asked if this was my first-time taking test.

I responded by saying, "Yes, isn't it yours?".

"No, this is my second time," he replied.

This would not have been a big deal; except he made the highest grade on the class test. You know how there is always a "know it all" in the class? This was him. I thought to myself if he did not pass the first time, I am sure I will not either. I became discouraged and more nervous than I was before I saw him. Before we could enter the test room, we had to empty our pockets and store our cell phones. It was getting real. It was about 10 of us in a small room with cubicles. I am not much of a test taker and not one to stay in the same place for a very long time, so sitting there from 8-12 pm was going to be a challenge in itself.

The test began, and the question appeared on the screen. I remember staring at the question for about 5 minutes because I did not understand what they were asking. Suddenly the guy sitting next to me stands and shouts, "F*ck this! I'm out!" Everyone started freaking out.

I finally settled down and finished the test. When I walked to the front to get my results, I just knew that I did not pass. I was right, but on the bright side I only missed it by 6 points. I left the center feeling good. People kept telling me that I would probably have to take it more than once, so I was ok with my score. I decided to schedule my second attempt for the following Monday. This time I was not as nervous, just anxious. After taking it for the second time, I made a 69, missing it by 1 point. Although I did not pass, I still felt optimistic. I was sure I could make a 70 the next time.

That next week, I studied like never before. I even studied at night while cleaning my buildings. Instead of listening to music, I listened to the audiobook in my headphones. I was determined to pass it this time. I stopped posting and talking about being a realtor because I was having such a hard time passing the test. If nothing else, I had to pass because I did not want to let everyone down. After all of the extra studying, I took the test for the third time. Guess what? I failed again. The worst part was I made a 69 again.

I felt there was no way made a 69 two weeks in a row. I was angry, to say the least., I decided to give up. Once again, I was defeated with no direction or alternate plan. I felt like it was everyone else's fault but mine. I was telling myself they failed me because I was black. They just wanted my money. The instructor sucked. Every negative reason and person I could blame entered my mind. Then, I called my wife.

"I failed again, and I'm done. I quit."
I could not keep setting myself up for failure. It just was not worth it.

She responded in her blunt but supportive way, "Get out your feelings and go take it again."

She also suggested that I take some time off to get my head together, and like always, she was right. Between the stress of my other two jobs and lack of sleep, I needed to just step away for a few days. When she got home that evening, I was sitting on the back porch smoking a cigar trying to calm down. I was upset because I truly wanted to become a realtor. I was hungry for the opportunity and all of the benefits that came with it. As bad as I wanted it, it just seemed like it was not going to happen.

She sat down and asked, "How can I help?"

My initial response was, "You can take the test for me."

Of course, that couldn't happen.

"Did you really study all of the material or did you jump over certain chapters and topics?"

"To be honest, I am not reading all of the material; I'm just focusing on the things that I feel like I don't know," I responded.

"I suggest that you read all of the chapters. When you are done reading take the practice tests in the back of the book. You can even download the app on your phone and listen to the lessons during the day."

I listened intently, because I knew she was right once again.

"Why are you rushing through the test? You have four hours for a reason. When you get to a question that you don't know, save it and come back to it later." She suggested.

After getting my mind right, I followed her suggestions and took the test for the 4th time.

T. Mills, the Realtor

I remember it like it was yesterday. I was standing in the lobby of the test center, waiting to see if I passed or not. After standing there for what seemed like an eternity, the lady finally comes out of the back, smiles and says, "You did it!" This time, I finally passed!

I am so thankful for my wife for pushing me and teaching me how to study. If it had not been for that conversation, I do not think I would have had the courage to continue pursuing my dream of becoming a realtor. I made a 74, but you would have thought I made a 94. I walked out of that test center feeling like I just passed the bar exam. I could not wait to call everyone to tell them the good news.

Of course, my wife and mother were excited. It is nothing like having people that support you and your dreams. On the other hand, I remember texting my boys to tell them the good news, and their response was "about time." Now I know they were excited, but that's just how we keep each other humble. Now that the test was out of the way, it was time to celebrate.

That weekend I believe we went to every bar in Birmingham. It was a great feeling and accomplishment, but now it was time to get to work.

I was finished with the class but there were a few more steps I had to take before I was officially a realtor. After obtaining a real estate license, you must find a company to work under. You also have the option to get a broker's license and start your own company. Since I was new, I had to find a company to work with and utilize my license. There were only two companies that I was familiar with, Realty South, which is where I took the pre-license course and Keller Williams, which was the company where Gabriel worked. I decided to meet with the broker from Realty South first to learn about the company and to see what they had to offer.

The broker was very nice; however, their business model did not align with my goals. I felt like he was trying to sell me instead of getting to know me. However, meeting with Keller Williams was totally different. My conversation with the team leader, Jennifer Toomer, was just that, a conversation. We did not talk much about the company. Of course, she told me about all of the exciting things Keller Williams could offer however, we spent more time talking about family, the future, and growth opportunities.

I was amazed at everything Keller Williams could offer, not to mention I knew a few of the agents in that office that were very successful. I would like to say I signed with Keller Williams that day, but I did not. I actually met with Jennifer two more times before I joined her office. Although I liked Jennifer, Keller Williams was not the powerhouse in Birmingham that it is now. Realty South was the big dog in the city. After praying on it, I decided to hang my license at Keller Williams. Although Keller Williams was not a dominant brokerage in the city, Jennifer had a vision for her office, and I wanted to be a part of it.

I signed with Keller Williams in June 2015. I could finally say, "Terry, you did it!" After several months in class, taking the test 4 times, and meeting with several brokers, I was finally a realtor. I recall signing my paperwork with Jennifer and her walking me around to the broker's office to introduce me to the team. During one introduction she explained, "Rick, I would like you to meet our newest agent Terry Mills. He took the test 4 times, but he was determined to become a realtor."

Rick stood up and asked me a question. He asked, "What do they call the med student that finished school with a C average vs. the one that finished with an A average?"

I paused and said, "I have no idea."

He responded with a smile and said, "They are both called doctors."

He extended his hand and said, "Welcome to real estate."

I don't think Rick knew what that conversation meant to me. He basically gave me the green light to move past that chapter and just focus on becoming a realtor. Prior to that conversation, I was very insecure about taking the test 4 times. I was not sure if I was going to make it in real estate because I barely got in. We laugh about it now and believe it or not, during our office's career night, Jennifer actually uses me as an example. She tells them my story to let them know even if they do not do well on the test, they can still be successful. It is kind of flattering.

THIS TOO SHALL PASS

After a couple of months, things were starting to look up again. I was finally living out my dream of being in real estate. Two months later, my sister-in-law and her husband kept their promise and allowed me to help them find and purchase their first home. Things were going great. I still had my job as Probation Director, and the janitorial service was doing well. What more could I ask for?

However, things would soon change. Nothing could have prepared me for what was about to happen. I was driving down the road one day, and my supervisor from the probation office called, "I have some bad news."

My mind started racing through every possible bad thing she could tell me. Was I in trouble? Was I about to lose one of my accounts? It was even worse.

"The company is losing money, and we are shutting down. Your last day will be November 13th". She explained.

Ironically, that was Friday the 13th. Are you serious? Shutting down? Now what? At that point, I had been with the company for nine years. We never experienced any layoffs or pay cuts, so to hear the company was closing, that was unbelievable. She informed me that I was only getting a severance check equal to six weeks of pay.

I became angry.

After nine years of service, all they could offer was six weeks of pay!?

After she hung up the phone, I did not know how to feel. It seemed like every time I would take two steps forward I had to take three steps back. There I was at a crossroads again trying to determine which way to go. I had only been in real estate a few months and was still learning the business. Until real estate picked up, my plan was to focus back on the janitorial company and pick up more buildings to clean. But "When it rains, it pours".

Only a few weeks after being told I was getting laid off from my day job, I received a call from the office manager in one of the buildings we cleaned. They informed me they were no longer satisfied with our service and wanted to use another company. Great, I said to myself. I was so frustrated that I decided to give the business up altogether. I just did not care anymore. I was tired of feeling like a failure and not being able to get ahead. In less than 30 days, I went from making six figures to trying to figure out how I was going to pay my bills.

I sat in church the following Sunday, confused. I was prayed, asked God why this was happening to me. He answered. During my pastor's sermon, he made the statement, "So what you got laid off! You didn't have the courage to quit and do the job that you really wanted to do anyway." That message hit me like a ton of bricks. I knew I had not told my pastor that I had just gotten laid off, so that had to be God's way of telling me things would be alright. I left church that day feeling refreshed and inspired. Pastor Craig was right; I would have never quit that job. I was on salary, could work from home, and as long as my region was profitable, my boss did not bother me. I had finally received the clarity I needed. Real estate was what I was supposed to be doing, not cleaning bathrooms nor running someone else's company. It was time to step out on faith and do what I was called to do.

In a perfect world, I could tell you the next six months were easy. Difficult does not even describe it accurately. The words painful and heart wrenching are more fitting. The last check I received that year was my severance from my job. After taxes, I only had enough to pay the bills for two months. Even though I was dead broke, no one knew it. Not even my wife. I would get up every morning, put on a shirt and tie, and report to the Keller Williams office like I had a million dollars in the bank. I realized sitting at home, feeling sorry for myself was not going to make me a successful real estate agent, so I might as well go to the office and work. I had several people that were interested in purchasing a home, but timing was off. Some wanted to wait until they saved more money, or improved their credit score I knew the money was coming, I just could not pinpoint exactly when. Realtors are 100% commission, which means we do not get paid until a client closes on a house. Although I was busy working as a realtor from July 2015 to December 2015, I only had one closing, and that was my sister-in-law and her husband.

    I am thankful that my wife was still working and able to manage our household bills. However, I still had to take care of my bills. After a couple of months of not making any money, the bill collectors started calling. We had just bought our house, had three car notes, and my wife was pregnant. That period of my life was beyond stressful. For years, I have always been the early bird gym rat. One morning when I left the gym, I decided to stop by Walmart to pick up some milk. While checking out my card was declined. My heart dropped to the floor. I couldn't believe it. I did not even have enough money to pay for a gallon of milk. I quickly grabbed my debit card from the cashier and walked to my car with my head down. I had never been so embarrassed in my life. I remember just driving around that morning in total disbelief. I felt like I had hit rock bottom. To add insult to injury, things continued to fall apart. I was driving my dream car, a pearl white 750 BMW, I also owned a black on black Dodge Ram truck that I loved just as much. Since I did not have any money coming in, I could not pay either car note. I finally told the bank to come get the truck; I just could not afford it anymore. I refused to give up my BMW.

After months of dodging bill collectors, I had to do something. Although real estate was starting to pick up. I was not making enough to catch up my bills. I finally decided to file for bankruptcy. I just could not deal with people calling and threatening me every day. I was embarrassed about it.

It was actually the smartest thing I could have done. Bill collectors could not call me anymore, and I did not have the stress of trying to pay bills. I finally could put all of my focus on real estate. When I did that, great things started to happen. In January 2016, I had four closings and made 12k. I remember going to the bank, and instead of depositing the checks, I cashed them. I asked the teller to give me all $100 bills. I went home and stared at the money and reflected over the previous months. Just a few months prior, I filed bankruptcy, and now I was holding a miraculous blessing from God. I went on to sell 41 homes that year and won the Rookie of the Year award, and I have not looked back.

THE MARATHON CONTINUES

I am sure after learning that I helped 41 families purchase homes my first year in real estate, one would assume that I knew what I was doing. In actuality, I did not have a clue. As I stated earlier, my first deal came from my sister in law and her husband. The other 40 were just blessings from God. I remember waking up every day, trying to decide what I was going to do. I did not have a job, so I had plenty of idle time. Just a few months earlier, I was complaining about having to get up at 2 am to go to work, and now I had nothing to do. I pulled out of the garage every morning asking God to get me out of the trap that I had put myself. Well, be careful what you pray for.

It is funny how your life can change in just a few months. When I first started at Keller

Williams, I did not have my own office. They provided areas in the building where new agents could come in and work. I figured if nothing else, I should get up, go to the office, and see what the other agents did. Maybe I could pick up something from the seasoned agents in the office. Even though I just finished real estate school, I still did not fully understand my job. The pre-license course was all about legal terms and math. It did not teach me how to be a realtor at all. Being in the office and observing everyone was simply intriguing. Everyone would walk around with headphones talking on the phone all day. I remember thinking to myself is this a real estate office or a call center? Who are they talking to? What are they talking about? Well, it was only one way to find out.

   I pulled one of the agents to the side and asked him to explain who he was calling all day. To my surprise, he was an open book and showed me his entire system. He had a website that would capture leads, and once they were captured, he would follow up with them to see if they wanted to buy a house. When you visit sites such as realtor.com or Zillow to search for a home and find one that you like and want more information, the site will prompt you to register or provide your contact information. After that, an agent would call you to see how they can help. I thought to myself, that was genius, and I need to do that. The problem was it was very expensive. Some agents were spending thousands of dollars a month to get business. There was no way I could afford to do anything like that.

There I was, dressed in a shirt and tie, driving one of the nicest cars in the parking lot, and in the middle of bankruptcy. The discouragement was starting to sink in again. If I couldn't afford to buy leads, how was I going to be successful in real estate? I had to figure out another way to get business because buying leads was not an option.

That weekend, my friends and I went out to eat and catch up with each other. We called ourselves "The Real Husbands of Birmingham." I know it is corny. It was always a great time when we linked up. Everyone could not wait to hear how things were going with real estate. Prior to getting into the business, we would always talk about investing and flipping homes so they could not wait to pick my brain. I started to explain that the business was not what I expected. Although I was still new, I did not really understand how people got business. I told them about the website that all the agents were purchasing leads. I also explained that because of the cost, that was not an option for me. I needed to come up with a way to get my name out that did not cost a lot of money. A few ideas were thrown around, but nothing really appealed to me. At the end of the night, someone took a picture and posted it to social media. The caption said, "The Real Husbands of Birmingham are back at it again". That post received roughly 200 likes and several comments. That just blew my mind! I could not believe that 200 people would like a picture of some guys just sitting at a bar. I was relatively new to social media and did not understand the power that it had. I had just started Instagram and Facebook accounts a few months before I started the pre-license course. I figured it could help me in sales, but now it was time to take it more seriously.

    The first thing that I needed to do was increase my friends on Facebook. But how would I do that? What was the first step? I figured the easiest method would be adding all of my friends' friends. My goal was to make these people my future clients, so I needed to get in front of them. That night when I got home, I logged onto Facebook and went to my wife's page. She had been on Facebook for years and had tons of friends. I just started adding them as my friends. For the next few days, I would continue this process until I increased my friends and followers. Now, I needed to plan things to post. I had only been an agent for a few months, so I did not have many real estate related things to post. I would just think of random things and hope that it would catch people's attention. To my surprise, it did.

Eventually, people were reaching out to me every day, asking questions about real estate. Every time someone had a question, instead of just answering them via social media, I would have them come into the office to talk. At the end of each consultation, I would ask if they would agree to take a picture so I could post on social media. It did not matter to me if they actually bought a home or not. It was free marketing! Plus, it gave me the opportunity to get in front of people to sell myself. Most of these were first-time buyers. They did not know much about the home buying process, and honestly, neither did I. I knew enough to get people started. After doing this for a few months, my phone started ringing off the hook! People would call saying, "I received your information from my friend who said you are helping him buy his first home." With each new client, I would repeat the same process. Invite them into the office for a consultation and close with a picture and caption, "Congratulations to this family! They are on their way to becoming homeowners! If you would like to be next call me at..." The feeling was amazing. I was finally feeling like a realtor. I did not realize it, but I was developing what eventually became my system. This is how I grew my business. It was simple but efficient.

After a few months, I was on fire, and I had closed several deals. Just when I thought things could not get any better, they did. I accomplished something that would change my career forever and solidify me in the real estate industry. One of the drawbacks of being a part of a real estate brokerage is agents must split their commission with them. For instance, when we close a deal, we do not get to keep the entire commission. A portion of it goes to the brokerage. In return, we get essentials like training and technology. At Keller Williams, they give their agents an opportunity to earn 100% of their commission. Their term for it is called capping. The way it works, we must sell at least two million dollars' worth of real estate during our calendar year. Your calendar year goes from the month that you joined the company through the next 12 months. Mine is from June to the end of May. I did not realize it, but only a small number of agents actually cap, so it is kind of a big deal.

During my rookie year, I capped in only six weeks. This was something that had never been achieved in that office. When I first received the news, I did not think much of it because I was just hustling trying to get back on my feet. My Team Leader, Jennifer, called to congratulate me. She explained that I set an office record. In the history of their 15 years, no one had ever capped that fast. "You should be proud!" she congratulated me.

That night, I went home and just took it all in. I was so busy working that I did not have time to stop and look at what was happening. God was showing me that this is what he intended for me to do. Real estate was my calling. It was only a few months earlier that I was struggling to pass the real estate exam, and now I was setting records. It just goes to show that anything is possible with hard work and dedication. As the year went on, and my business continued to grow I was blessed to help several families achieve the American dream of homeownership, and in return, I won the Rookie of the Year award.

THINK LIKE A CEO

It was the first Monday of January 2017 and time to get back to work. When I arrived at the office that morning, all of the hype from the holidays was gone, and everyone had returned to business mode. I remember sitting in my office staring at my Rookie of the Year trophy, reflecting on how great the previous year. It was amazing how far I had come from just a few months earlier. If someone would have told me that I would have been able to accomplish these things, I would not have believed it.

I kept thinking about the story that Rick, our broker, at the time, told me about the medical student when I first joined the company. It did not matter if he/she finished medical school with a "C" average or an "A" average, he/she was still a doctor. He was right. It did not matter that I had to take the real estate exam several times. I was not only a realtor; I was becoming a successful realtor.

My achievements from the previous year proved it.

In addition to personal satisfaction, it was a blessing to help people achieve their dream of owning a home. Several of my clients were not only first-time homeowners, but many were the first in their family to own a home. These are the stories that made the job even more rewarding.

My wife and I were recovering financially, so one would assume everything was all good. Not exactly. My first year was amazing, but now I had to do it again this year. The problem was I really did not know what I did. On the outside looking in, it appeared that I had it all figured out. But in reality, I did not. Most of it was just pure hustle. Just like in our cleaning business, I did not have a business plan. I just worked hard, and things happened to work out. However, that same model was not going to work in real estate. I just could not afford to relive that scenario. In order to remain successful, I needed to become purposeful and implement systems. I did not want to just sell real estate; I wanted to manage and execute a business. I have always heard that success does not motivate people; the fear of failing does. That was incredibly true in my situation. The thought of not being able to repeat the success of my rookie year scared me to death. I was determined to figure something out.

Later that day, I decided to go to my team leader Jennifer to ask for some advice. I explained to her that 2016 was amazing, but I had no idea how I was going to duplicate it again. She looked at me and said four simple words, "You need a coach."

Now I played sports my entire life, so my initial thought of a coach clearly could not be the same thing she was talking about. I asked her what she meant by a coach. "What kind of coach?" She said, "a business coach." Someone that would help me not only put a business plan together but help me obtain my goals. This sounded good because, at the time, I did not have either. She then went on to tell me that she also had a business coach, and it was the best investment she could have ever made. I had not thought about it, but most successful people have coaches. Even star athletes have coaches that they hire outside of their head coach to help them improve in certain areas.

Jennifer suggested that I set up a meeting with Retha. Retha was the coach that we had in the office. At first, I was not on board. The thought of paying someone to tell me what to do just was not appealing. I thought the point of becoming an entrepreneur was to be your own boss, not take orders from anyone else. This was my mindset. Little did I know hiring Retha would eventually become the best investment I could have made. When I got home that night, I talked to my wife about the conversation with Jennifer about hiring a coach. I just knew she was going to be totally against it. We were just getting back on our feet, so I assumed she would not want me creating any new bills. Again, I was wrong. Shockingly, she supported the idea.

"If it is going to make you successful, let's do it."

Let me add, having a supportive spouse is priceless. Your support system is EVERYTHING. Having someone to have your back, hold you accountable, and encourage you when you are no longer able to push yourself is invaluable. Being a business owner is great, but it comes with stress because all of the decisions are made by one person, the owner. It is great to be able to have someone to talk things over. I decided to reach out to Retha to see what her coaching program was all about.

The next morning when I arrived at the office, I actually bumped into Retha in the hallway. Her very first words to me were, "Why don't you have a coach? What? You think you're all that?" I was like WHAT!?! Who is this chick talking to? She later explained that she knew that would get my attention, and she was right. She knew that I would not have taken her seriously if she came at me all nice and kind. Well, she certainly had my attention. We eventually sat down later that day to talk about her program. I was blown away with her proposal. She explained some of the things that she could do for my business things like helping with creating my brand, setting my sales goals, and creating the systems to achieve them. This was perfect because those were all of the things that I did not have. Although deep down I knew she could take me to the next level, I still was not convinced. Well, honestly, I just did not want that level of accountability.

The thought of having to report to someone weekly did not sit well with me. Like I stated earlier, the point of being your own boss was not having to report to anyone. Over the next few weeks, I decided to speak with some of the top producing agents in the office about their thoughts on hiring a coach. I was shocked to find out that most of them also had business coaches. After hearing that, I changed my mind. If I was going to make it in business, I had to get out of my comfort zone and start doing things differently.

The definition of insanity is doing the same things over and over and expecting different results. If I did not want my real estate business to fail like my cleaning business did, I was going to have to start thinking differently. It was time to level up. I decided to step out on faith and hire Retha as my coach. Outside of having a great business relationship, Retha and I ended up becoming very good friends. Now we are more like brother and sister, but it did not start out that way. She has a very strong personality, and so do I. The first few sessions did not go so well. She would assign a task for me to do, and I would spend the session telling her why it would not work. She wanted me to do things her way, and I wanted to do things my way. We laugh about it now, but I remember one coaching session she actually kicked me out of the room. She said if you are not going to listen, I will just give you your money back and you can get out of my office. I remember thinking to myself. I hired her, how could she fire me? After a few days, I put my pride aside and decided to listen. She was right; the point of hiring her was to help make me successful. If I was not going to trust her, it was a waste of time for both of us. A few months went by, and I was starting to see improvement in my business. I was no longer just hustling. I was running a business, unlike the previous year when I just randomly made up things to do every day in hopes that it would generate business. I had an actual daily routine and knew what I was supposed to be doing every day. Not only did implementing these systems increase my business, but it removed the insecurity that I felt at the beginning of the year.

As my business increased, so did the time I spent working. You must remember that I filed bankruptcy, so I was hungry. It's nothing like having your dream car taken away from you. The image of the tow truck driving away with it still motivates me to this day. I was determined to never be broke again, so I wanted all the money I could get. Although that idea sounded good, it would come with a price. During one of my coaching sessions, Retha made the statement that I worked too much. She asked how my wife felt about it. Of course, I did not think it was a problem, but it was. After talking to my wife, I found out that she felt like I was putting work first. Our first-born Trace was only a few months old, and she needed more help around the house.

I explained to her that I was working hard for them.

"Money is not everything, Terry. We need you here sometimes."

Although I did not want to hear it, my wife and Retha were both right. I worked every single day. Anytime someone wanted to meet with me or see a house, I would make myself available. There I was thinking the purpose of hiring a coach was to help increase business, but instead she helped me learn that having a family life was just as important. All I knew how to do was hustle. I really did not know how to address this issue. All I knew was my phone was ringing, and I was not going to turn away new business. Retha generated a schedule to help simplify things. Monday was my administrative day. This was the day I could only deal with paperwork and administrative tasks, no appointments. During the rest of the week, I would generate leads in the morning and show houses in the afternoon. My wife would usually have a day off during the week, so Retha would allow me to use that as my flex day to either work from home or take my wife to lunch.

At first, I was scared that my production was going to decrease, but it did not. My business was running smoothly. But most importantly, I was able to achieve a work/life balance. I realized hiring a coach was the best investment I could have made in my business. To this day, Retha remains the machine behind the scene. At the end of 2017, I was able to accomplish some amazing things. I had the privilege of serving on our office's agent leadership council, which is basically like the board of directors. We work with the team leader to discuss the office's budget, training opportunities, and implementation of policies to improve the market center. My sales increased as well. I actually surpassed my previous year by selling 52 homes and being recognized by Real Trends as being one of the top single agents in the state of Alabama.

For the Culture

I made it to year three and business was booming. Over the previous two years, I was blessed with the opportunity to help almost 100 families achieve the American dream of home ownership. My first year was really about learning the business and trying to figure out what I was doing. I would attribute most of my success that year to my sphere of influence and friends and family that simply wanted to see me succeed. The rest was just pure hustle and my desire to win. Year two was about finding my identity and proving that I was truly legit, for lack of better words, not just a one hit wonder. I would attribute that success to my business coach.

Going into year three, I had a totally different focus. It was not about me anymore. It was about being a trailblazer for those coming after me. It was not about how many houses I could sell or how many awards I received. I was now focused on opening doors and giving opportunities to others. I realized that I had opportunities in real estate that many did not have. I was a top producing agent in what is now the largest real estate brokerage in the state of Alabama. This meant I had the opportunity to learn from some of the best agents in the state. I actually have some mutually beneficial relationships with several agents in the office. However, there was one distinct thing.

Most of the top producing agents are not Black and their sales are of higher priced homes than mine. One important thing to remember is this is still Birmingham, Alabama. Historically, the world knows that diversity is not one of our areas of strength. Birmingham is different from other major cities like Atlanta, Houston, or Washington DC, where there is a large percentage of Blacks earning high salaries. In Birmingham, most of our successful African Americans are physicians, attorneys, business executives, as well as those working in industrial areas. This has resulted in a lack of Blacks purchasing homes in the higher price points or purchasing homes period.

Earlier this year, I was at our annual conference, The Keller Williams Family Reunion.

It is a time when all of the Keller Williams agents from across the country meet for a week of training and networking. Over the last few years, I have met some amazing agents, both black and white, that have positively impacted my real estate career.

One day, agents from Washington DC and I were discussing how different the housing marking is in all of our cities. One agent mentioned that he sold 60 homes in his very first year in real estate. I congratulated him because that was impressive. I remember how hard it was to sell 41 homes in my first year, so 60 was a major accomplishment. I started picking his brain to learn how he sold 60 homes in his first year. I also was curious about careers of his clients because the average price for a home in DC is around $500k.

The other amazing fact was this guy was only about 25 years old. He went on to explain that most of his clients had just graduated from college and had government jobs awaiting them or worked in the technology field. Credit approval wasn't an issue either, however, Birmingham is totally different. We are not the capital city, there are not as many government-based jobs in the area. There are people working in areas of technology like IT and programming, but my personal clientele of first-time buyers does not represent that particular group. Credit is also a major barrier with my clients. To put it in perspective, if five people express interest in buying a house, at least three of them will need to work on their credit score before they are able to purchase.

This is not to insinuate that my clients are not worthy of home ownership but just to show the financial disparities that many face when they seek the "American Dream". Birmingham's price points are significantly lower than other metropolitan cities. There is a smaller percentage of African Americans in higher tax brackets in Birmingham. The average price of my client's houses is around $170k compared to some of the other agents in my office that are around $250k. This means they can sell fewer homes but make more money. I sold 52 houses in my second year. This was one of the highest numbers in the office. However, I was only ranked number 8 that year because my volume was lower.

Agents are ranked by volume, not by the number of houses we sell. At 52 houses, I sold about 8 million in volume, which is good. However, the number one ranking agent sold around $15 million in volume, but only sold about 30 homes. As you can see, I have to work harder just because my clients' price points are lower. Although credit and price points are challenges, they are not the biggest. The biggest challenge that we are faced with is changing our clients' mindsets.

Most of my clients are not only first-time buyers; most of them are the first to buy a home in their family. Many of them did not believe they could purchase a home because they had not been exposed to people who have. I have had several people tell me that they were scared to call me about purchasing a home because they did not believe they would qualify. I did not realize how real this limiting belief was until one day my friends and I, "The Real Husbands of Birmingham," were having a discussion.

My friend Freddy asked, "Tuck, have you ever thought about what you are doing? You are really changing people's lives by helping them purchase homes."

At first, I thought he was just blowing my head up, but he was really serious. Freddy said the only reason he bought a house was because I was in real estate. Prior to that, he was content with his previous situation.

He said, "Just think about how many of your friends that you put in houses. This is bigger than you now, and you should take it more seriously."

Until then, I really did not think about it. In my first two years, I helped several of my close friends and family purchase homes.

My friend Will shared the same sentiments, "Bro, I never thought I would purchase a home either."

Both of these men have very good jobs. This limiting belief was all in their mind. He reminded me that his mother never bought a home, nor did her mother, so when he and his wife closed on their home, it was truly a big deal. After that conversation, I realized that this was bigger than me. When I first got into real estate, I just looked at it as an opportunity to make money. After conversations like this, I totally switched my focus. It was not about me anymore, and I felt obligated to help as many people as I could achieve the American dream of owning a home. In my opinion, these are some of the reasons we do not have many top-producing Black agents in our city. We have to work twice as hard just to be recognized as a top producer.

Although I am a competitive person and would like to be the best at everything that I do. Awards and recognition are not as important to me as helping and educating blacks on the importance of good credit and the benefits of home ownership. A couple of years ago I attended a leadership conference in my church. The theme of the seminar was, Are you using the talent that God gave you to change the world? As I sat there that day I had to ask myself the same question. Was I using the talent that God gave me?

At first I wasn't sure what my talent was and then it hit me. Real Estate, God gave me this platform to educate people about the power of real estate. After that conference I started looking at real estate like a ministry. I no longer was focused on recognition and awards. My new focus was helping people change their lives and real estate was the just the platform. We are all looking for a way to make more money and become financially stable however the answer is right in front of us. Over the last two centuries about 90 percent of the world's millionaires have been created by investing in real estate. I know several people that have good jobs and make good money. However, they are throwing a lot of it away paying rent instead of investing it in a house. I understand that there is a time and a season for everything however, living in an apartment should be temporary. I personally have lived in apartments, but I eventually had to make the decision to stop throwing money away.

Before my wife Tiquela and I got married we lived in an apartment for 3 years. Our rent started out at $700 a month but before we moved out it had increased to over $900 a month. We sat back and added up how much money we spent living there and the number made us sick to our stomach. We spent almost $30,000 in rent and did not have anything to show for it. Another big mistake that I have seen people make is paying cash for everything. Some people do not have a checking account. I have several friends that say they do not want any bills. I understand that however when they go apply for a mortgage it's hard to get them approved because they do not have any established credit.

One suggestion that we give them is to get a secured credit card to start building credit. A secured credit card requires you to put your own money down to open the account and pay yourself back while establishing credit. A lot of people just don't know the home buying process and some are even afraid to try to purchase. Many of us were not taught the importance of saving money, establishing credit, and investing. A lot of people have misconceptions about the credit requirements for a mortgage. Some do not know that you may qualify with a 620 credit score or anything about the no money down programs. Which is why my team and I offer free buyer consultations to anyone that wants to learn about the home buying process. We also host free home buyer workshops in which we cover all of the phases of the home buying process from, establishing credit, saving money applying for a mortgaging and buying your dream home. Although credit and price points are challenges, they are not the biggest. The biggest challenge that we are faced with is changing our clients' mindsets.

As I continued in my third year in the business, sales continued to increase, and so did my brand. I do a lot of marketing on social media; people began to see the success I was having. I soon found out that success also brings on responsibility. Many began suggesting that I open my own brokerage. They did not understand why I was still working at Keller Williams.

For a while, I ignored the noise until two successful local brokers got my attention. I was at a real estate event when they pulled me to the side and made the statement, "You need to open your own brokerage for us." Now, these two agents would be considered competition. I did not understand why they would encourage me to open a competing brokerage. How would that help them? One explained, "We need you to do it for the culture." We only have a handful of Black owned brokerages, but we have a plethora of Black agents. The other broker then explains that she admired what I was doing and knew that I had what it would take to be successful as a broker. Over the next few weeks, that conversation stuck with me, and I had to do something about it. As much as I wanted to ignore the conversation, I could not. Blacks are the biggest consumers, but we do not own anything. This is one of the reasons it is so difficult for Black people to buy homes. Most of us start off in debt and do not have any assets to help us buy anything. I instantly started to think about my sons. I was a successful realtor, yet I did not own anything. If I died today, all they would hear was that their dad was a successful real estate. So what? That would not pay for college or help them purchase their first home. That conversation weighed heavily on my mind. If for nobody else, I needed to do it for my sons. After some thought, I decided that I was going to leave Keller Williams to start my own company. Because of the relationship that I had with my team leader Jennifer, I scheduled a meeting with her to discuss what I wanted to do. I explained that I had nothing against her or KW, but I felt I had an obligation to do something bigger. I wanted to open more doors for Blacks by helping them create more opportunities for wealth. After explaining my point of view, she responded by saying, "I don't blame you for wanting to do more but leaving to open up a brokerage isn't necessarily going to help you accomplish your goal." She also stated, "You just haven't seen anyone at Keller Williams doing anything to that magnitude in Birmingham."

She then told me about her friend named Bo, who was doing amazing things in Washington, DC. I was shocked because I had heard of him and all of his amazing accomplishments, but I did not know that they were friends. A few weeks later I received a call from Bo that would change my perspective. Bo was Black, so he understood exactly where I was coming from. He explained that I did not need to change my desire. I just needed direction. He invited me to spend time in his offices to see the types of organizations that he owned. When I arrived, I was blown away by the magnitude of his business. It took me a day to understand his organization chart. He owns several Keller Williams offices with over 1k agents. In addition, he owns several businesses, such as a commercial real estate company and a single-family development company. He explained that he started as a single agent just like me and, in just 15 years, was able to build an enormous enterprise that was worth millions of dollars.

When I got back to Birmingham, I was more motivated than ever. I wanted to be just like Bo. I figured if he could do it, so could I. He gave me a copy of his organization chart as a blueprint. This would give me step by step instructions on what I needed to do to grow into an enterprise. The very first thing that he told me to do was grow a sales team. It was impossible to make the impact that I wanted to make by myself, so I needed business partners. Over the next few months, that was my focus. I am now blessed to work with an amazing team of agents to service clients in the Birmingham area. The next step is to take the capital from the sales and start investing in remodeling homes. We started our "house flipping" company, Legacy Development, LLC, in the Fall of 2019 and are currently working on our first project. I also had another goal. I have been an athlete all my life, so being healthy and in shape has always been a priority. We started a run club to not only help people achieve their fitness goals, but we also raise money to donate to various charities. All of these things are great, but the one that I am most proud of is the T. Mills Scholarship Fund, which was founded in 2019. In the Fall of 2020, we have committed to awarding $1000 scholarships to 6 deserving seniors. Each year, with the help of God, we will continue to enhance our reach and open doors for others

Trust Your Process

As I reflect on my life, I have been blessed to accomplish some amazing things. I have a beautiful family, thriving real estate business, and I am in good health. For the most part, there is not much more I could ask for. Now, these are all things to be proud of, yet the biggest accomplishments were the lessons I learned along the way. Most entrepreneurs are so busy grinding and trying to get to the next level that we never stop long enough to enjoy what we have already done, and more importantly, how we did it. As you can see, before every accomplishment that I made, adversity met me head on.

A few years ago, I was asked to be the keynote speaker at a youth football team award banquet. I was asked to give a speech on motivation and overcoming adversity. Instead of giving them my story, I decided to talk about a famous basketball player.

Instead of telling them who I was going to talk about, I started off reading all the times that he failed, and they had to guess who it was.

"I've missed more than 9,000 shots in my career. I have lost almost 300 games. Twenty-six times, I have been trusted to take the game winning shot and missed. I've failed repeatedly in my life".

After reading this, I asked the kids who I was talking about, and no one knew the answer. Once I told them it was Michael Jordan, arguably the greatest basketball player of all time, they could not believe it. On the outside looking in, we never would consider Michael Jordan a failure, but he failed several times in his career. When he first tried out for the varsity basketball team, he did not make it. A few years later, he was drafted to the NBA in the first round. Once drafted, many said he was not going to be successful in the league, and he won the NBA Rookie of the Year award. Too often, we only hear about the success that people have obtained, but we never talk about their failures. The truth is failure is what drives us to be successful.

I never considered myself to be great at anything, but not being great is what forces me to work harder. All my life I have felt like the underdog not having any real advantages, and that is what drives me each morning that I wake up. Even going all the way back to high school football, I was not the best player on the team. I was considered undersized for my position. Instead of using that as an excuse, I was determined to play. My goal was to outwork everyone else so my coaches would notice me. Although I did not get a football scholarship, I was voted one of the team captains my senior year. In college, I really struggled. I started off being very intimidated, and honestly, I did not think I would ever finish. Despite my insecurities, I decided to stick with it. Although I had to change my major three times and almost ended up on academic probation, I was able to obtain my degree.

My career as a probation officer had its challenges as well. After not getting hired by the state and feeling like I wasted time getting a degree in Criminal Justice, I ended up having a successful career in the private sector. Although I was able to advance from probation officer to probation Director for Central Alabama in just a few short years, I was met with several challenges along the way. Early in my management career, I had an employee that filed a lawsuit stating that I wrongfully terminated her. She never came to work, but because I did not keep a good record of her attendance, our case was not that strong. A few years after that, while serving as the office manager for our Birmingham office, I was almost fired. One morning when I arrived at the office, the CEO of the company was there. At first, I did not think anything of it until he came into my office and stated that we needed to talk. I was told that my office had been losing money for months and they have decided to let me go. As you can imagine, I was in total shock. I did not see that coming at all. I mean, I was not even aware that we were not profitable.

I explained to the CEO that I did not even see the monthly P & L reports, nor was I informed that it was my job to keep up with the office's profit. My immediate supervisor, who at the time was the probation director, handled all of that. I never knew that was my job. After hearing my side of the story, I did not get fired. My supervisor was fired, and a few months later I was given his job. Just imagine if I did not stand up and plead my case. I would have gotten fired for something that was not my fault. In 2015, I decided to get my real estate license just to make some extra money. I would never have imagined that a few months later, I would get laid off, and real estate would end up being my full-time career.

Before every accomplishment, I was met with some form of adversity. I could have decided to throw in the towel and quit, but I decided to keep going. I was visiting with my grandmother a few months ago, and she asked me how it feels to be living the American dream. At first, I paused and just looked at her. I honestly thought she was being funny because she is silly like that. However, she was being serious.

She said, "You are doing great for yourself, and I am so proud of you."

Hearing that come from my grandmother was priceless. I responded by saying, thanks. However, I certainly did not feel like I deserved it. I mean, just a couple years earlier, I was going through bankruptcy and had all my cars repossessed, so how I was living the American dream?

She reminded me, "We all go through hard times, but they are only for a period, and trouble does not last forever. Life is a marathon and not a sprint, and we are not defined by one period of our life. The key is to keep going no matter what. Take me, for example, as a young mother, I was forced to leave my kids and move thousands of miles away just to get a job as a house sitter. Eventually, I was able to reunite with my daughters and retire from nursing."

My mother is another example of a person that overcame adversity. After graduating high school at the early age of 16, she was forced to postpone college for a couple of years after finding out she was pregnant with me. A few years later, she did obtain her college degree while working a full-time job and taking classes at night as a single parent. After years of having a successful career, life would happen, and she would resort to working in a chicken plant to make ends meet. She could have given up, but she did not.

Instead, she went back to school to obtain two nursing degrees and, in just a few short years, ended up becoming the Chief Executive nurse at Cooper Green Hospital here in Birmingham. We all have disadvantages and will be met with some form of adversity but who cares, nobody! We can either fall victim to our current situations or choice to defy all odds the choice is yours.

The biggest challenge in real estate is lack of inventory. I have clients ready to purchase and we cannot find them a house. Due to historically low interest rates we have several people ready to buy and increased number of people who are refinancing. It is a catch 22 motivating buyers to buy and sellers are staying in place at the same time. Sellers are keeping their homes because of the uncertainty in the economy and they may not have a home to purchase.

I recently revisited an idea I had before becoming a relator, flipping houses. I teamed up with one of the biggest flippers in Birmingham to create some inventory. This has been an amazing experience for both of us, and I am enjoying it, maybe one day I will write a book about it!

Acknowledgements

This book never could have happened without the love and support of a few special people.

First, I want to thank my beautiful wife, Tiquela for just being the person that she is. I would not be the man that I am today if it were not for your love and support.

I want to thank my mother, Deborah Andrews for your support, contributory details from my early childhood, and editing.

Many thanks to my grandmother, Eddie Mae Bryant for your unwavering support and for details of my family's history.

Special thank you to "my boys": Corey, Will, Joe, Chip, Byron, JeCorey, Freddie, and Justin, for keeping me inspired, humbled, and always having my back.

Thank you to the T.Mills Realty Group for keeping the business going while I focused on this project. The team members are Jennifer, Corey, Bobby, and my mother, Deborah.

Thank you to my business coach Retha, for always challenging me to dream big and teaching me the importance of having a work-life balance.

Thank you to Jennifer, Keller Williams Vestavia Team Leader/CEO, for always being supportive and encouraging; you were instrumental with the title of this book.

Made in the USA
Columbia, SC
03 October 2020